Amazing Patterns

ADULT COLORING BOOK

Sophie Justin

Colors Test Page

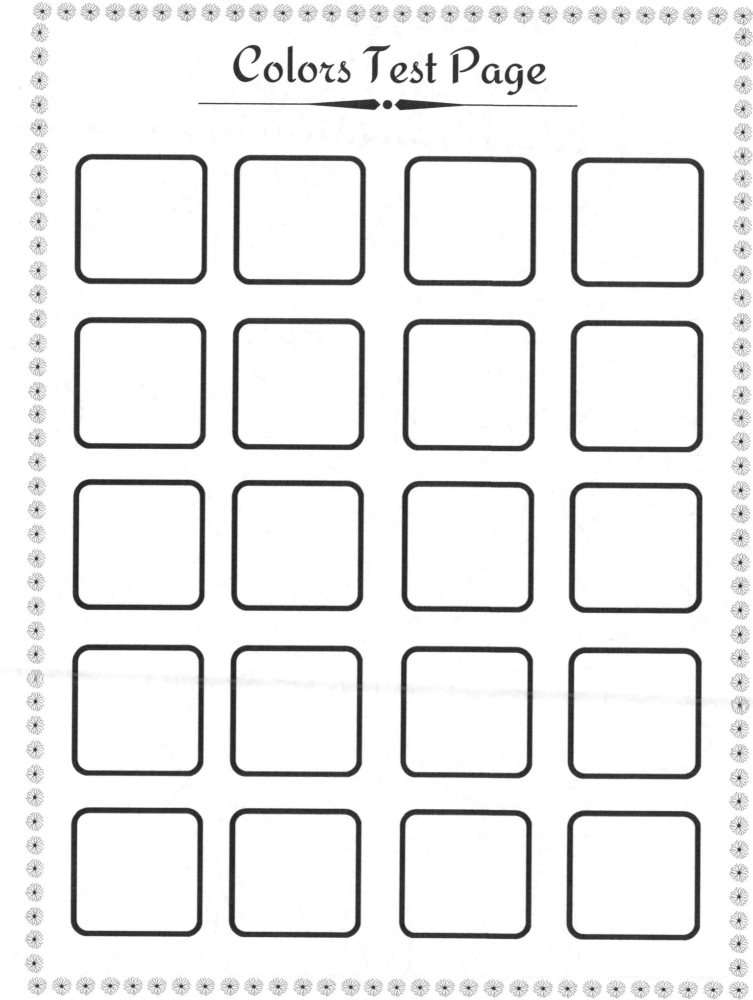

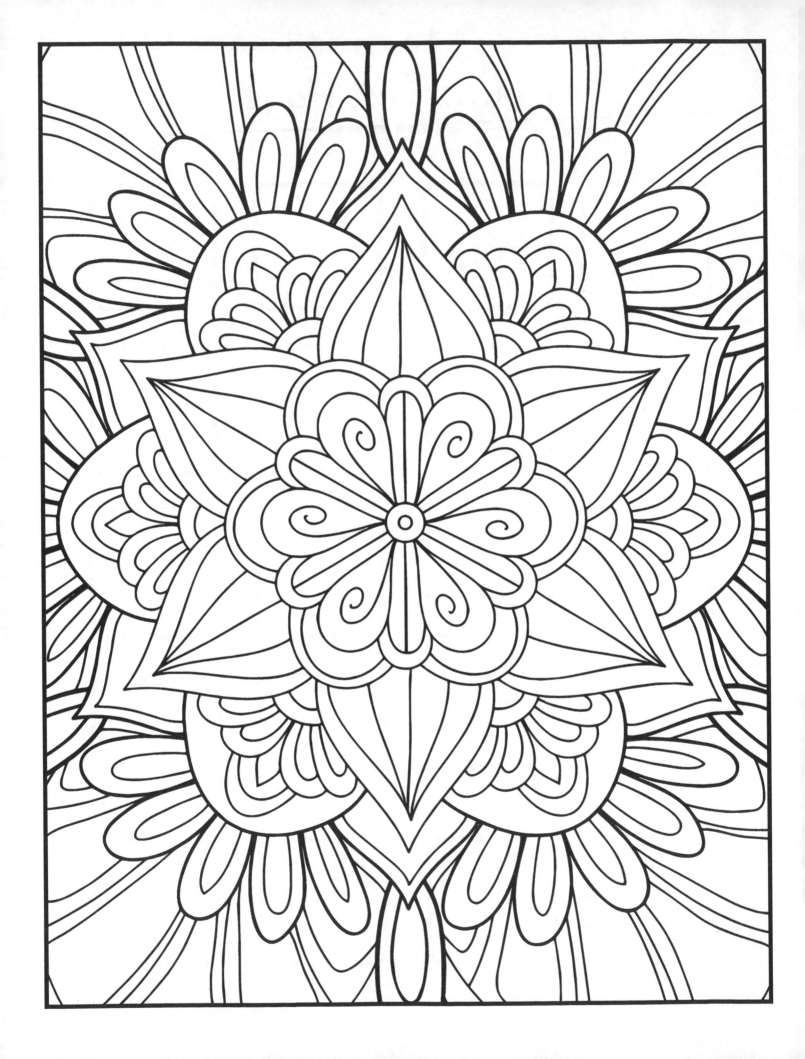

Create Your Own Patterns

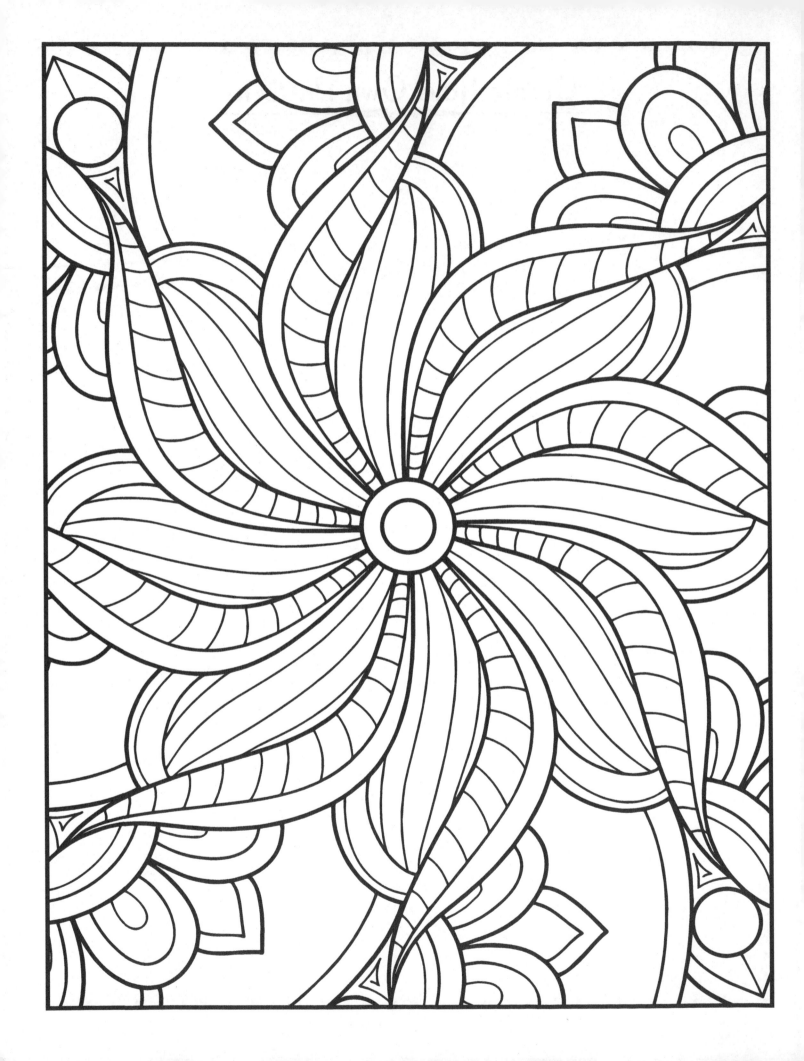

Create Your Own Patterns

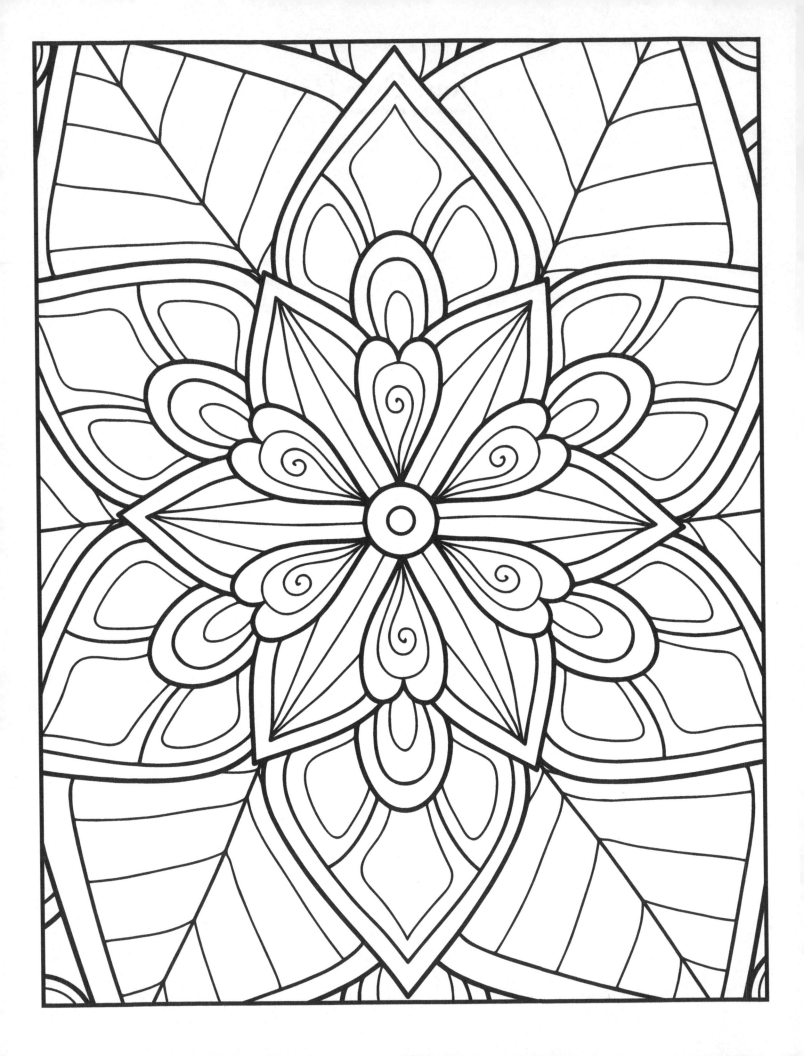

Create Your Own Patterns

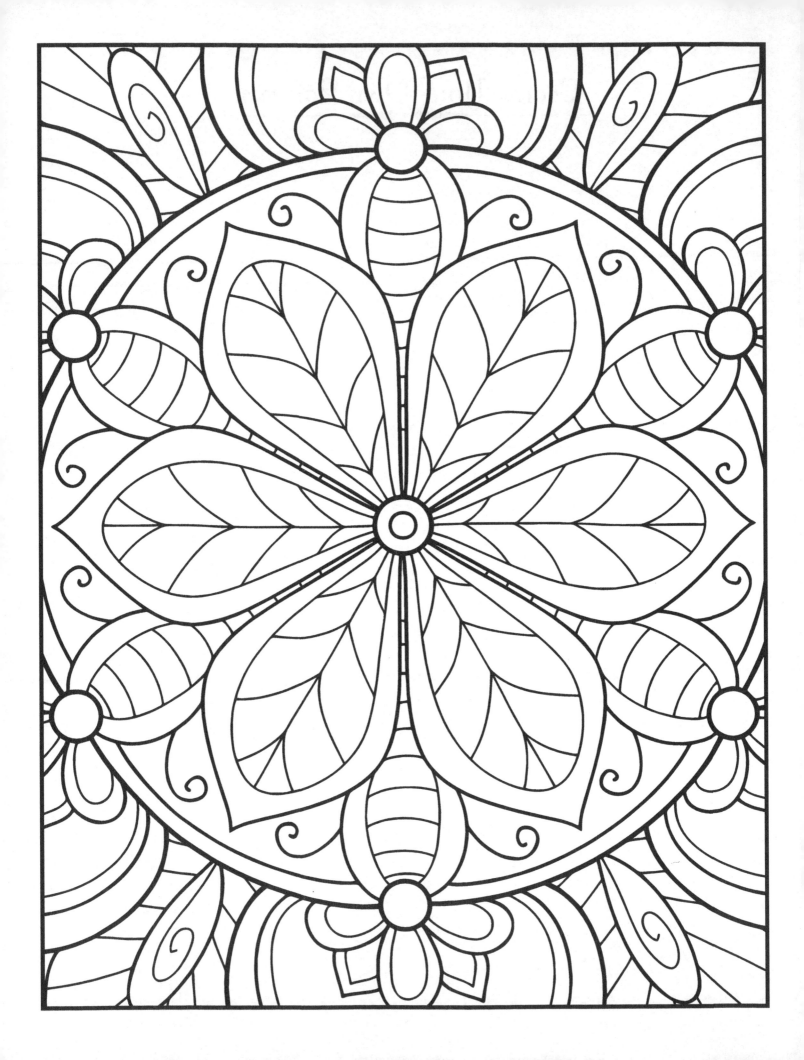

Create Your Own Patterns

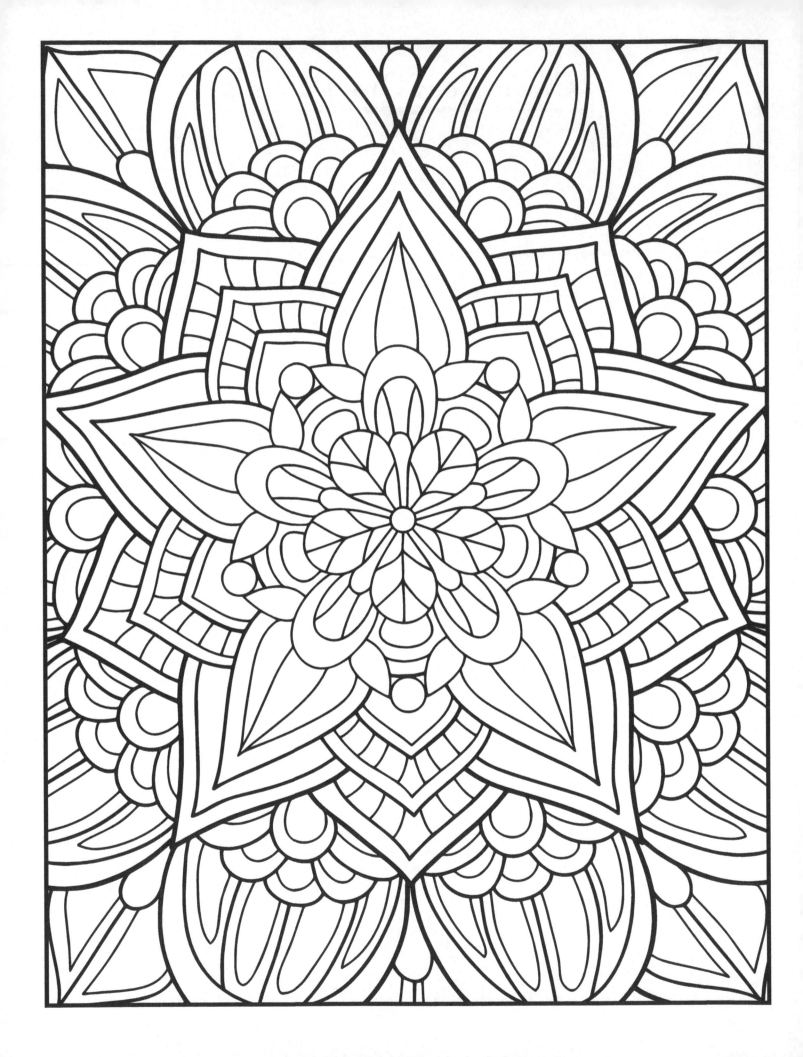

Create Your Own Patterns

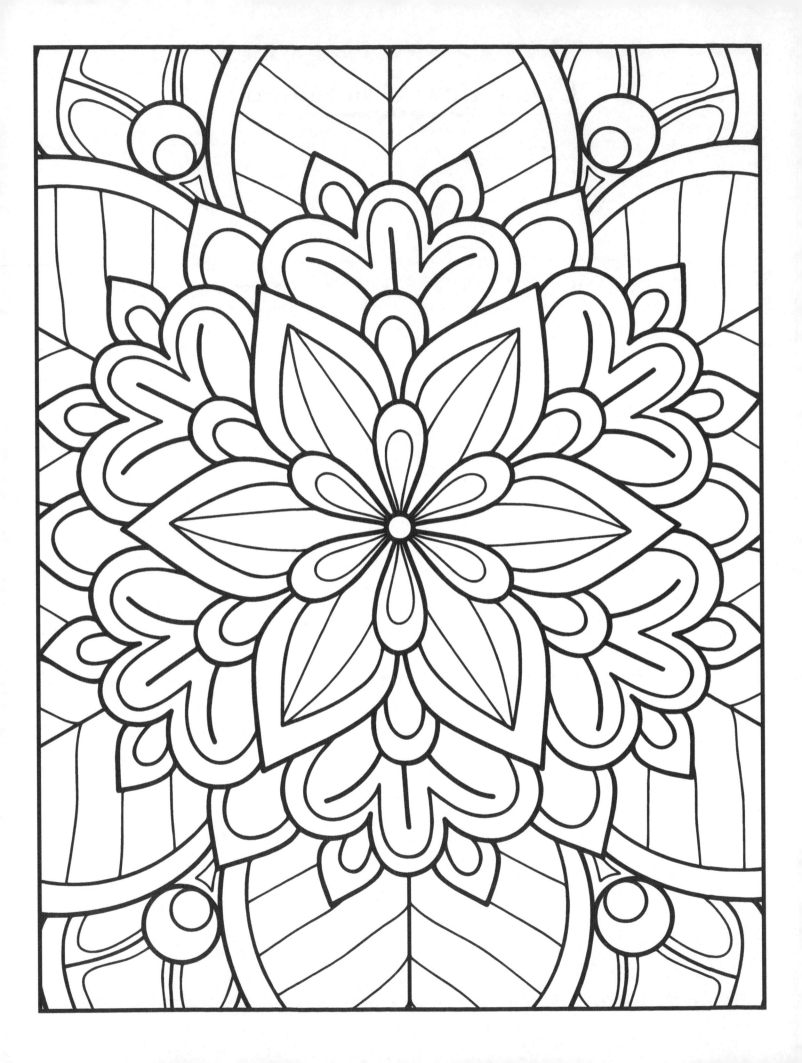

Create Your Own Patterns

Create Your Own Patterns

Create Your Own Patterns

Create Your Own Patterns

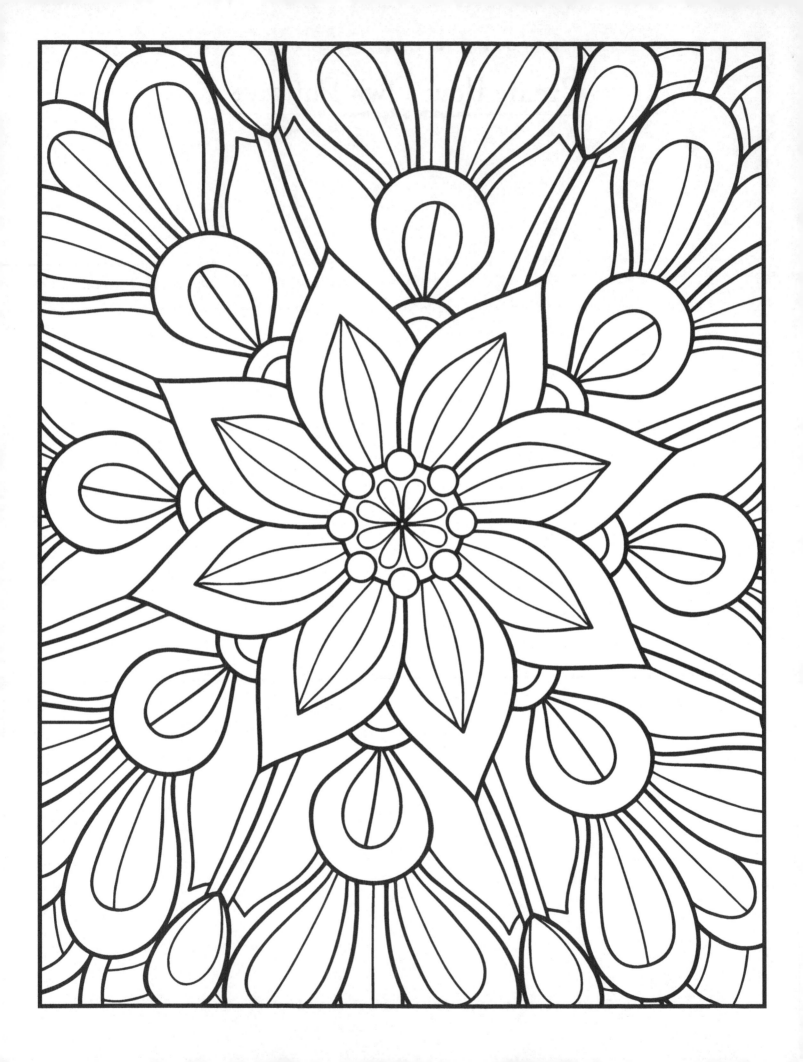

Create Your Own Patterns

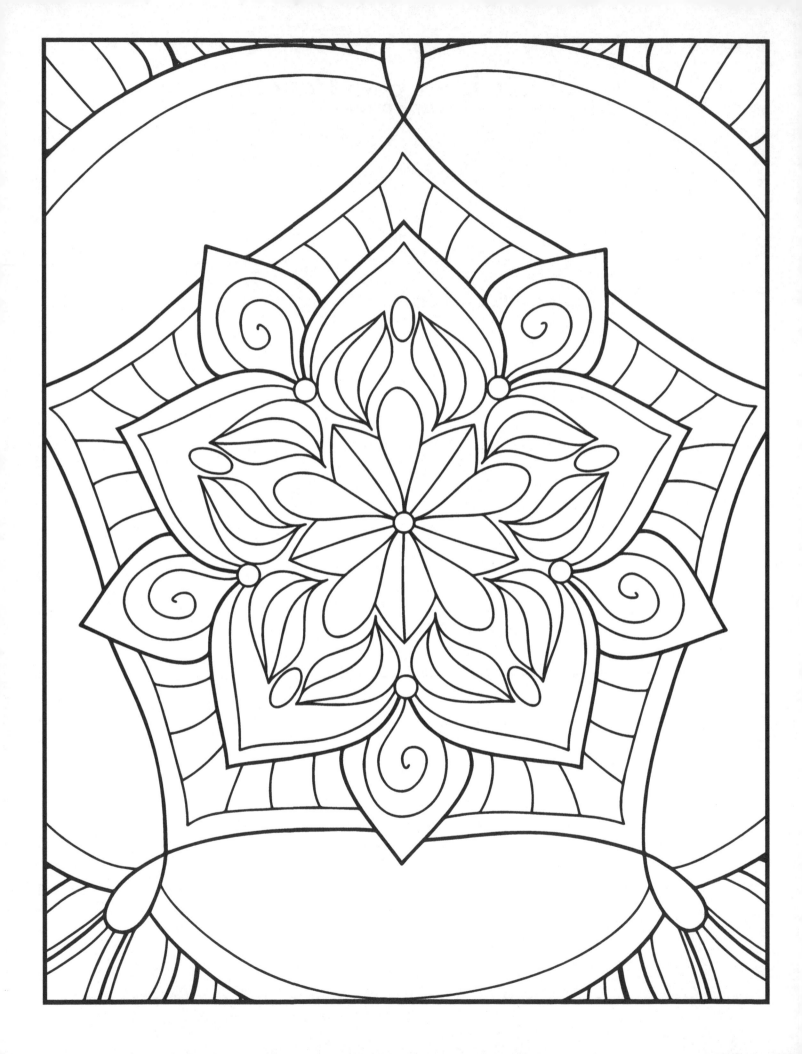

Create Your Own Patterns

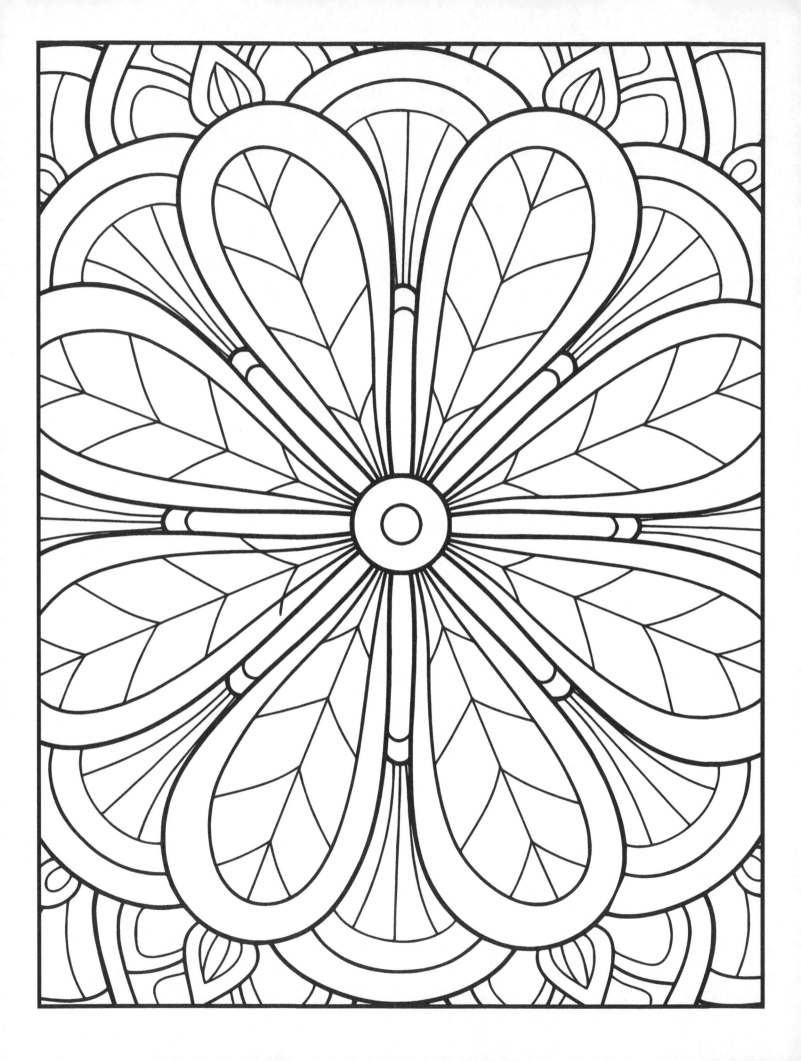

Create Your Own Patterns

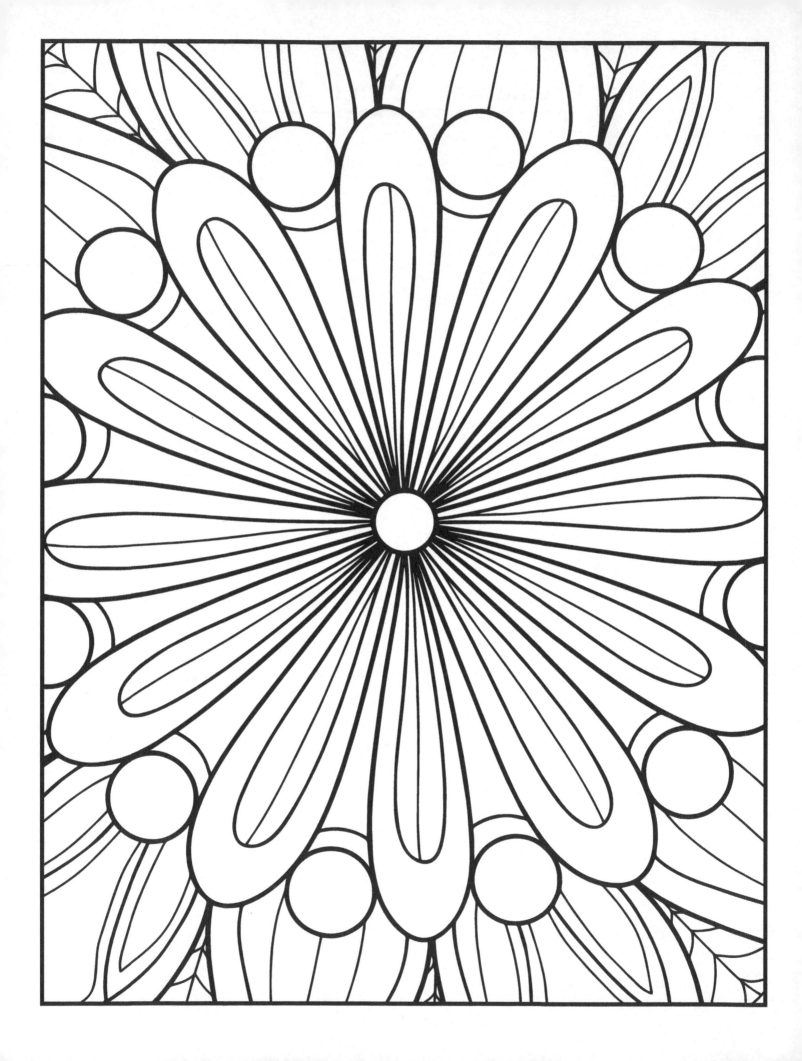

Create Your Own Patterns

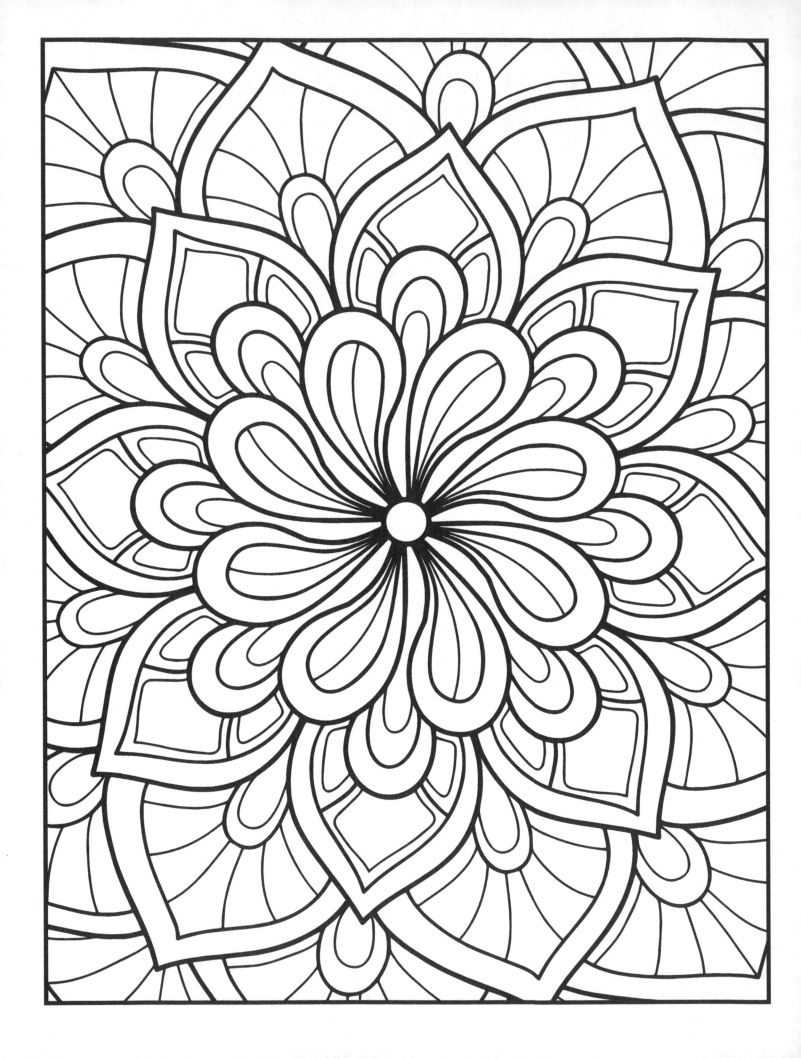

Create Your Own Patterns

Create Your Own Patterns

Create Your Own Patterns

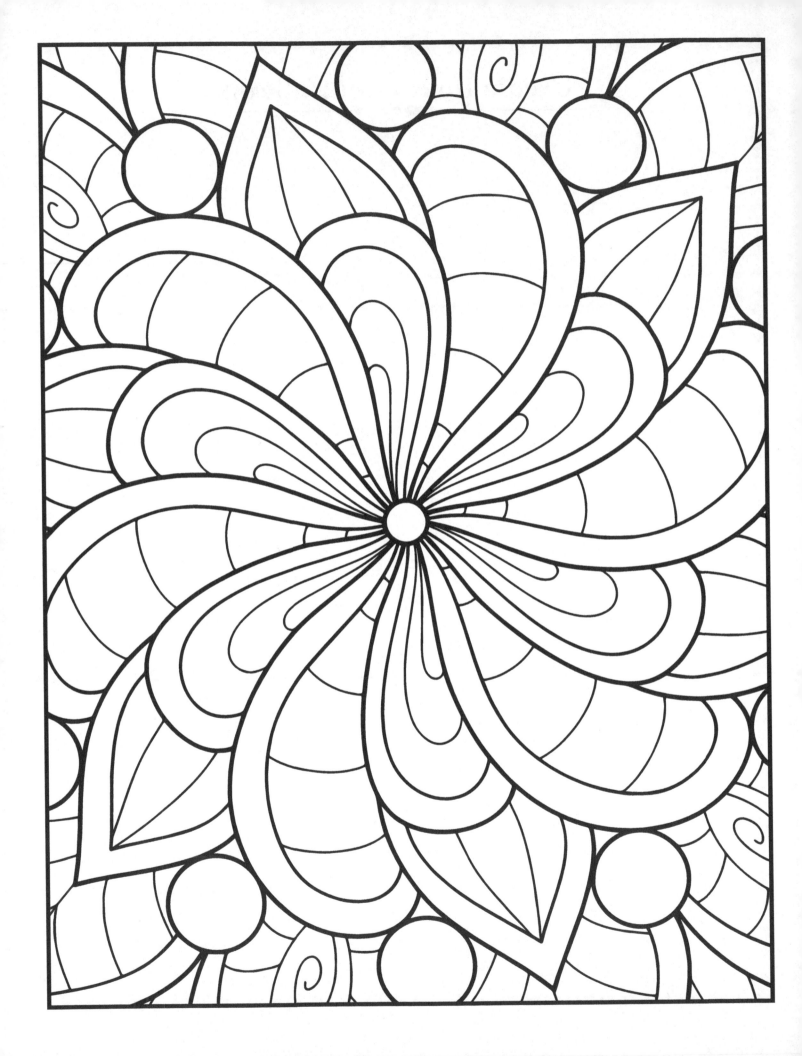

Create Your Own Patterns

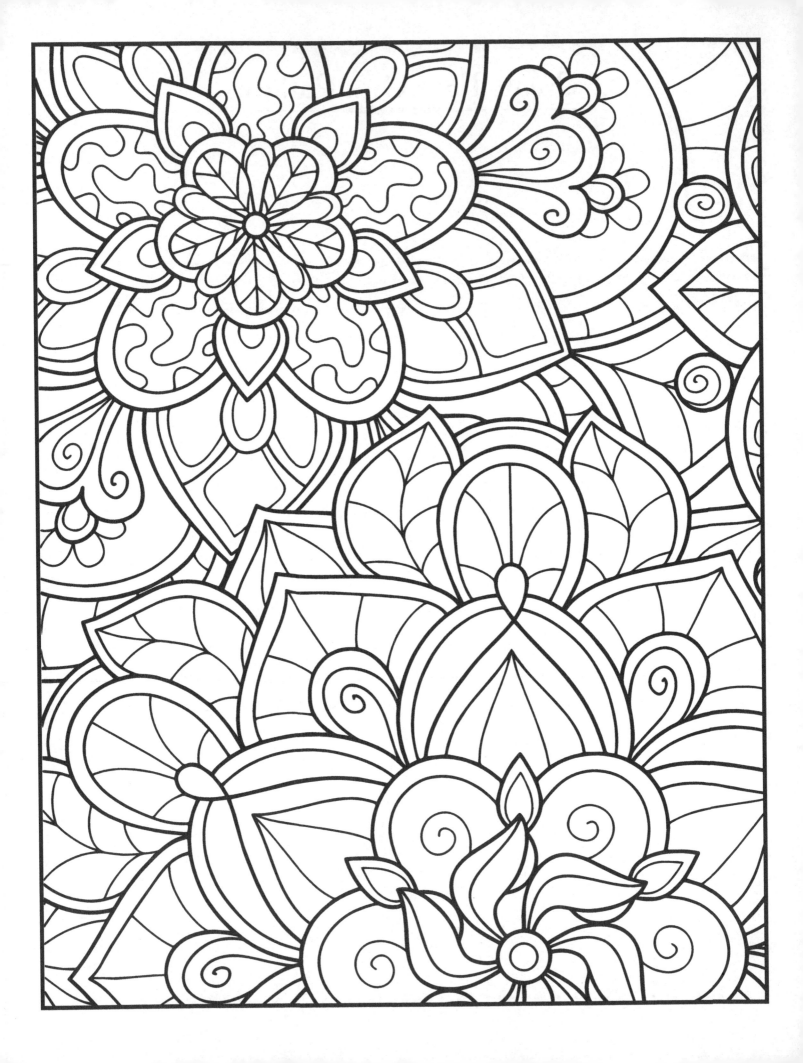

Create Your Own Patterns

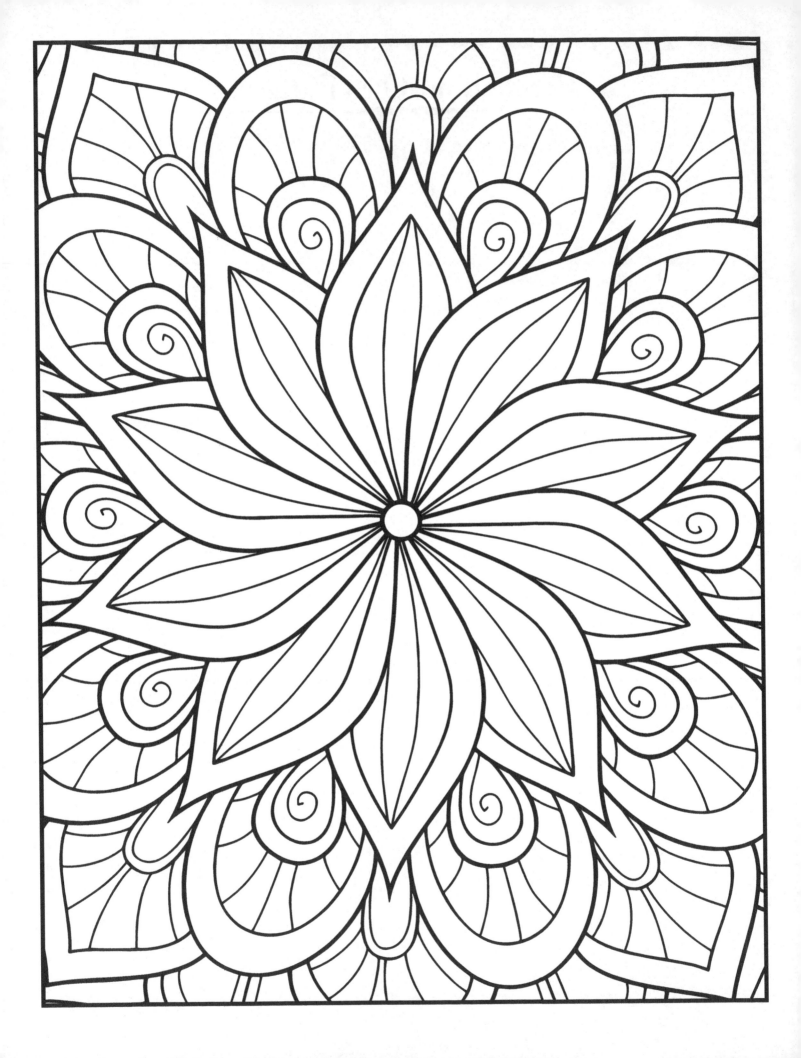

Create Your Own Patterns

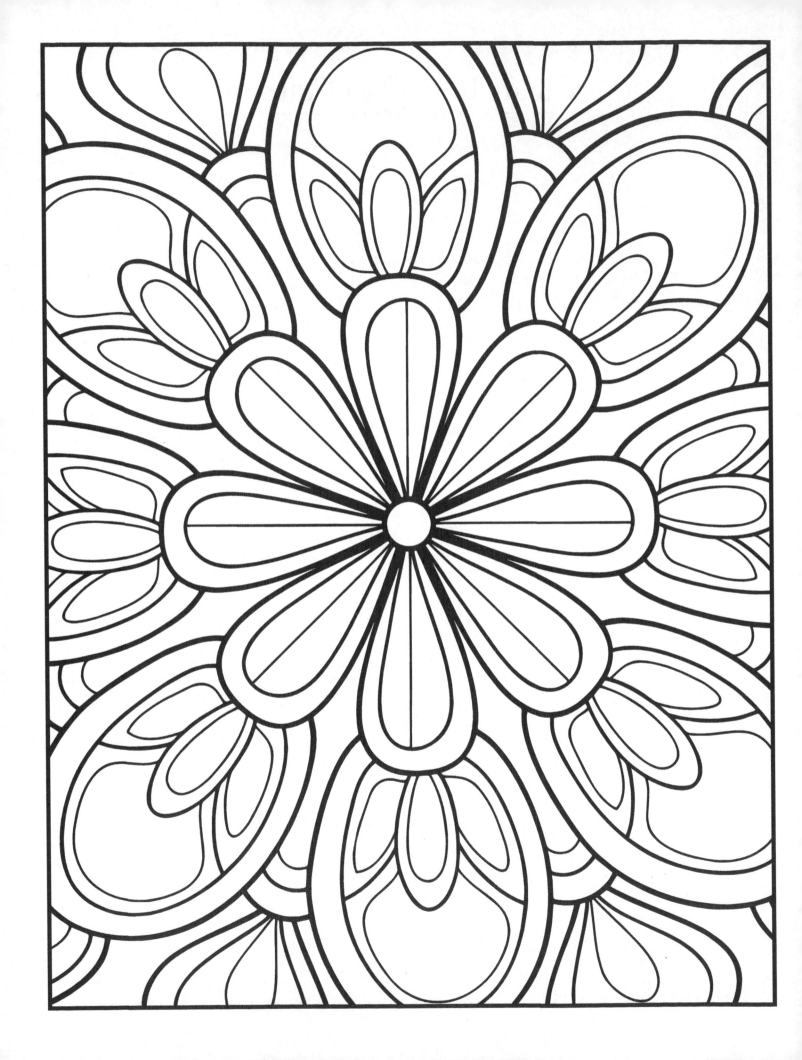

Create Your Own Patterns

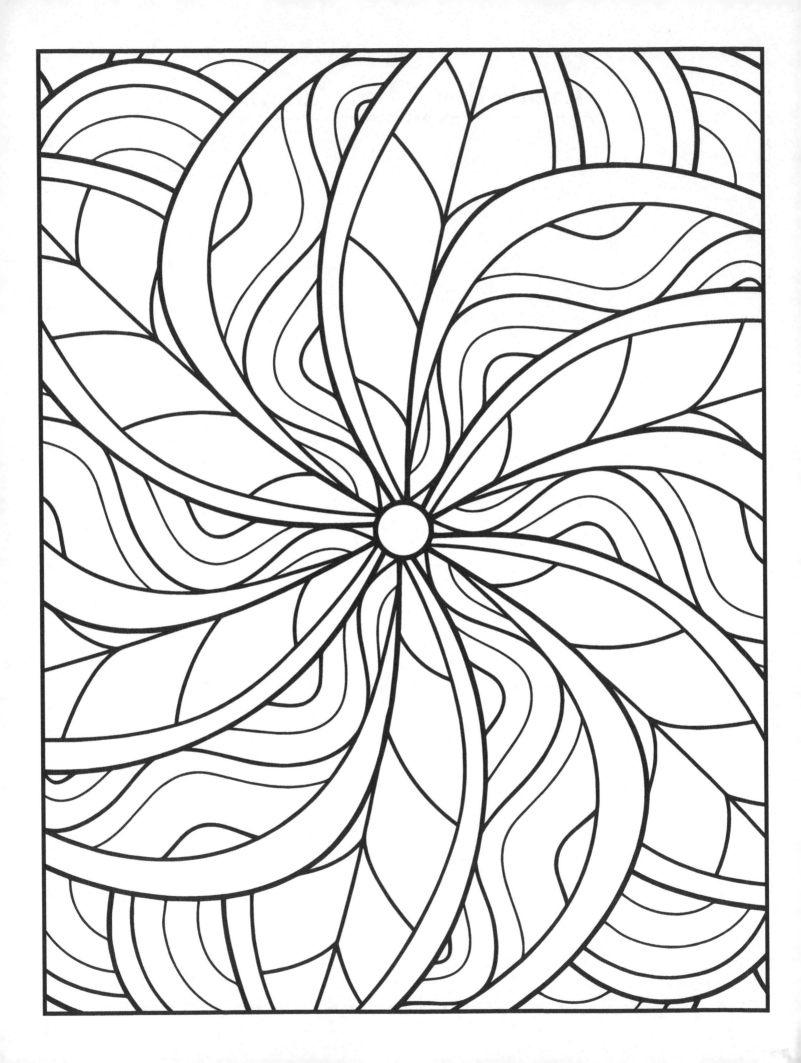

Create Your Own Patterns

Create Your Own Patterns

Create Your Own Patterns

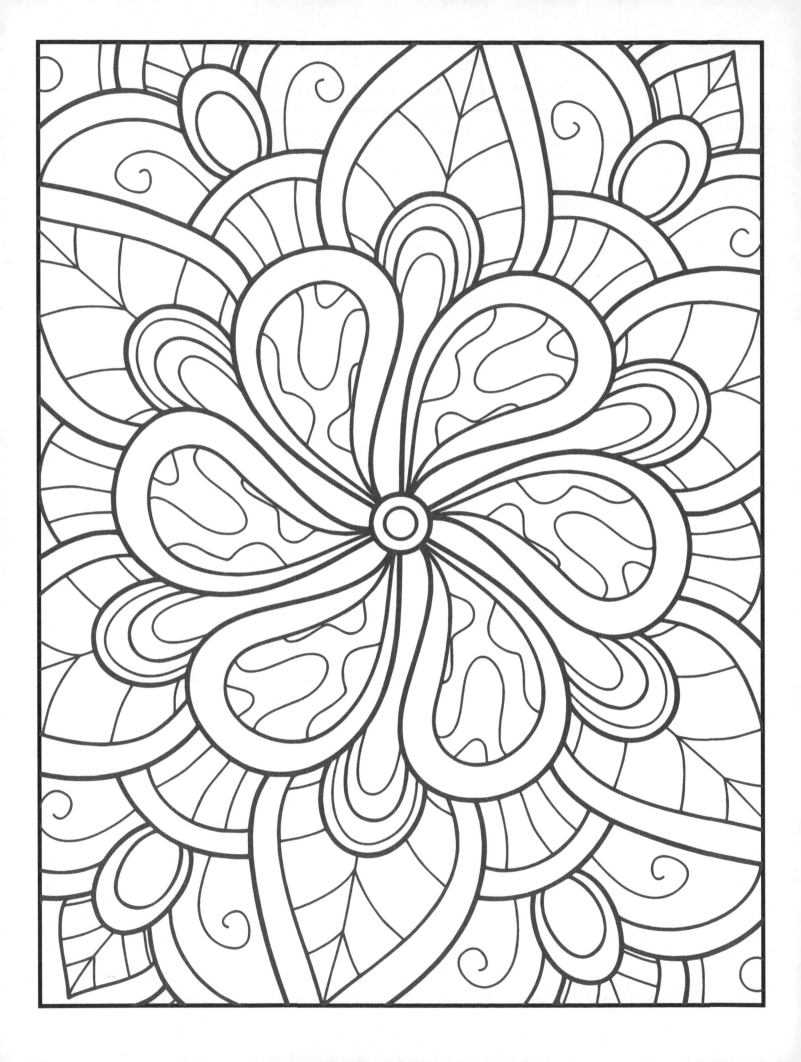

Create Your Own Patterns

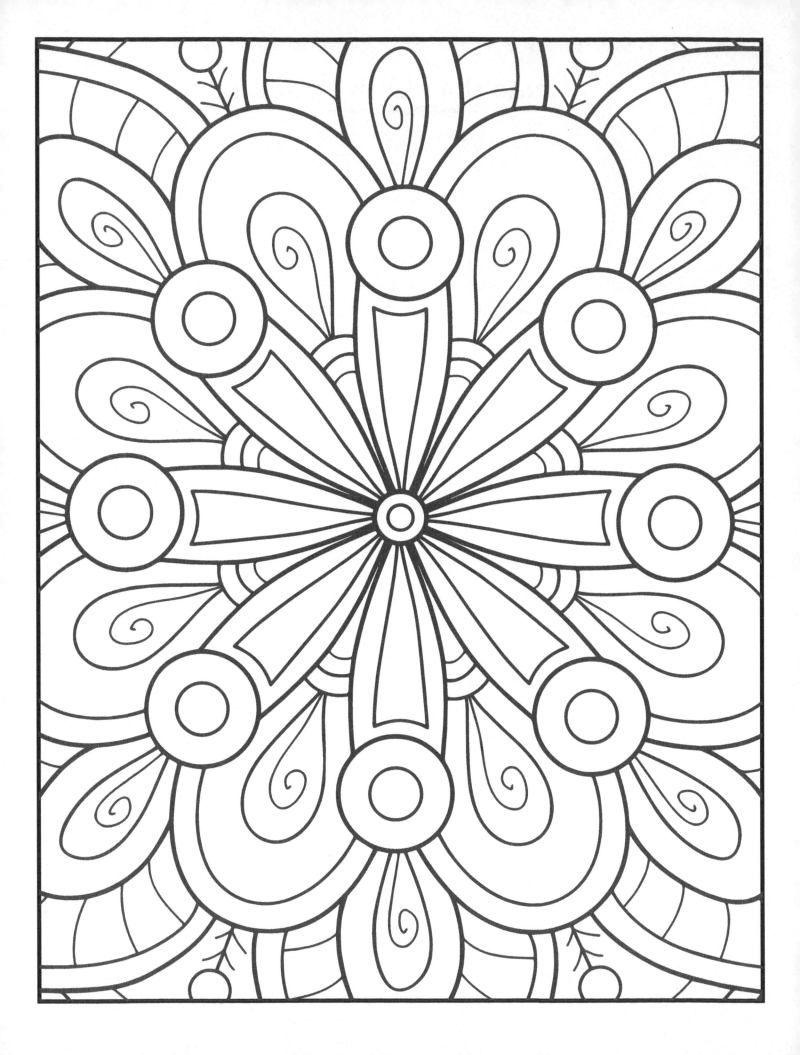

Create Your Own Patterns

Create Your Own Patterns

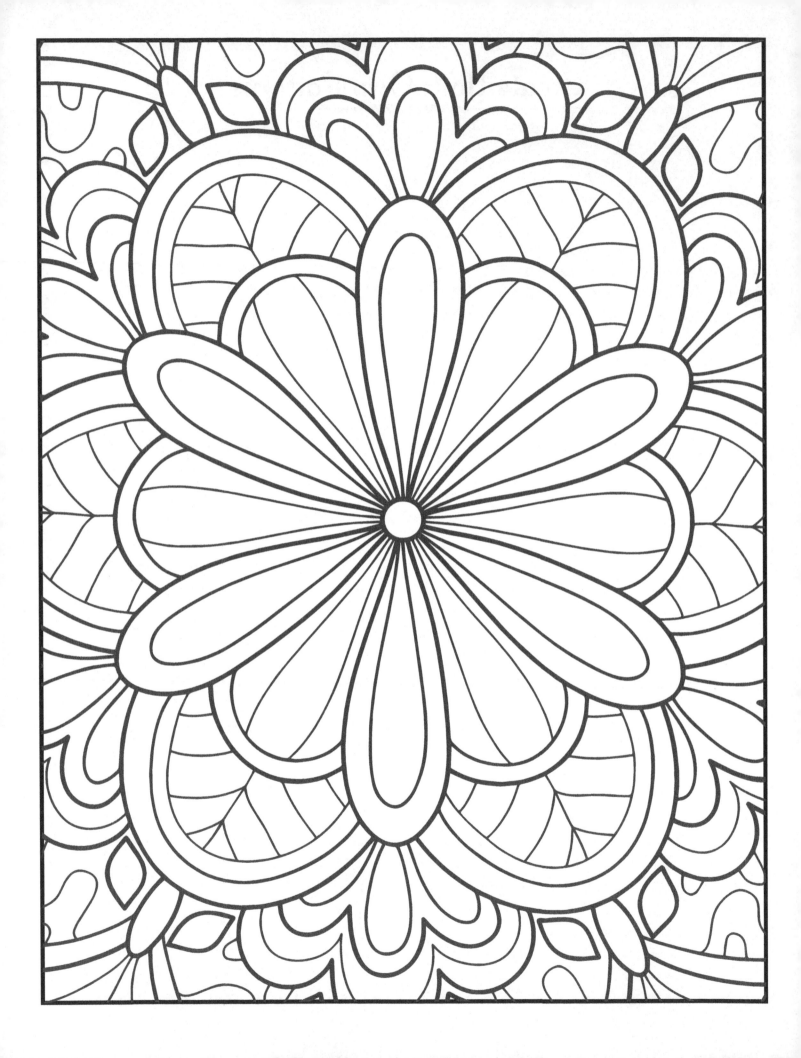

Create Your Own Patterns

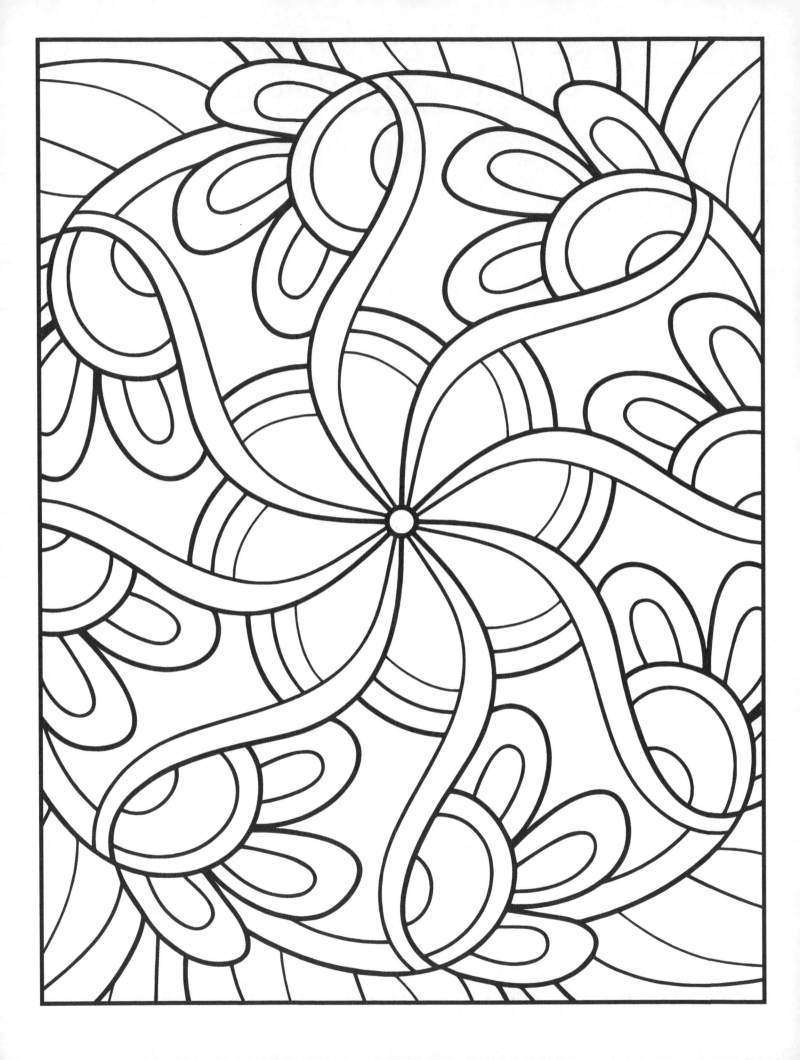

Create Your Own Patterns

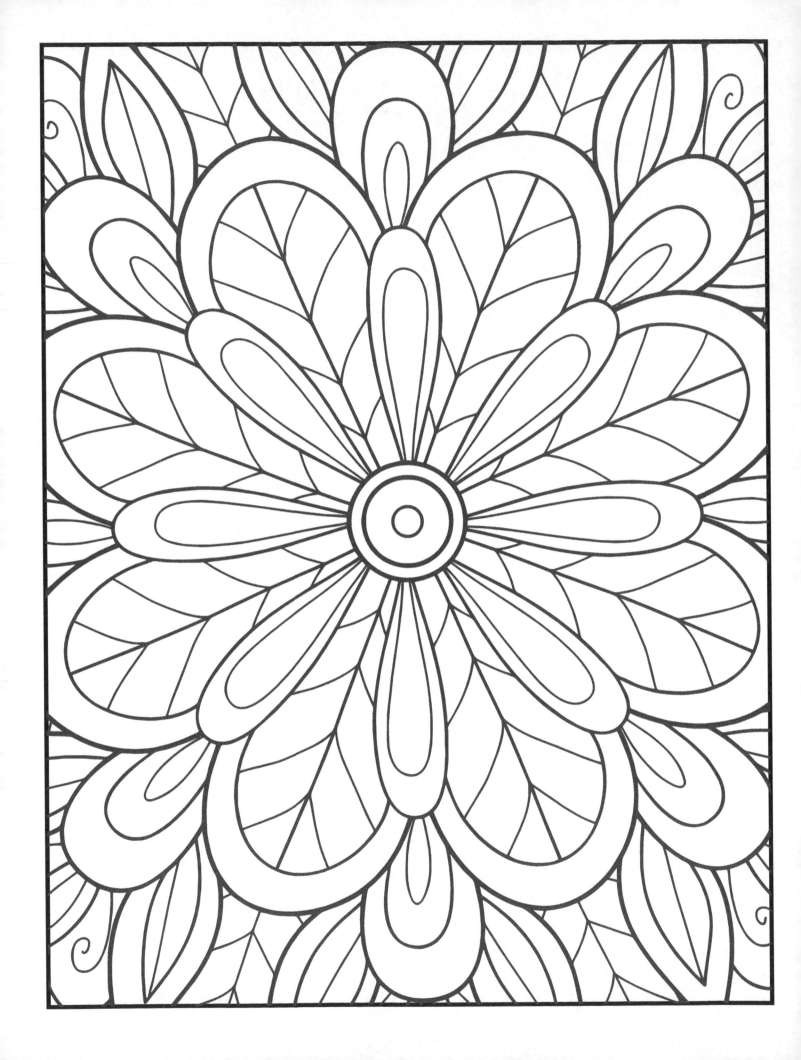

Create Your Own Patterns

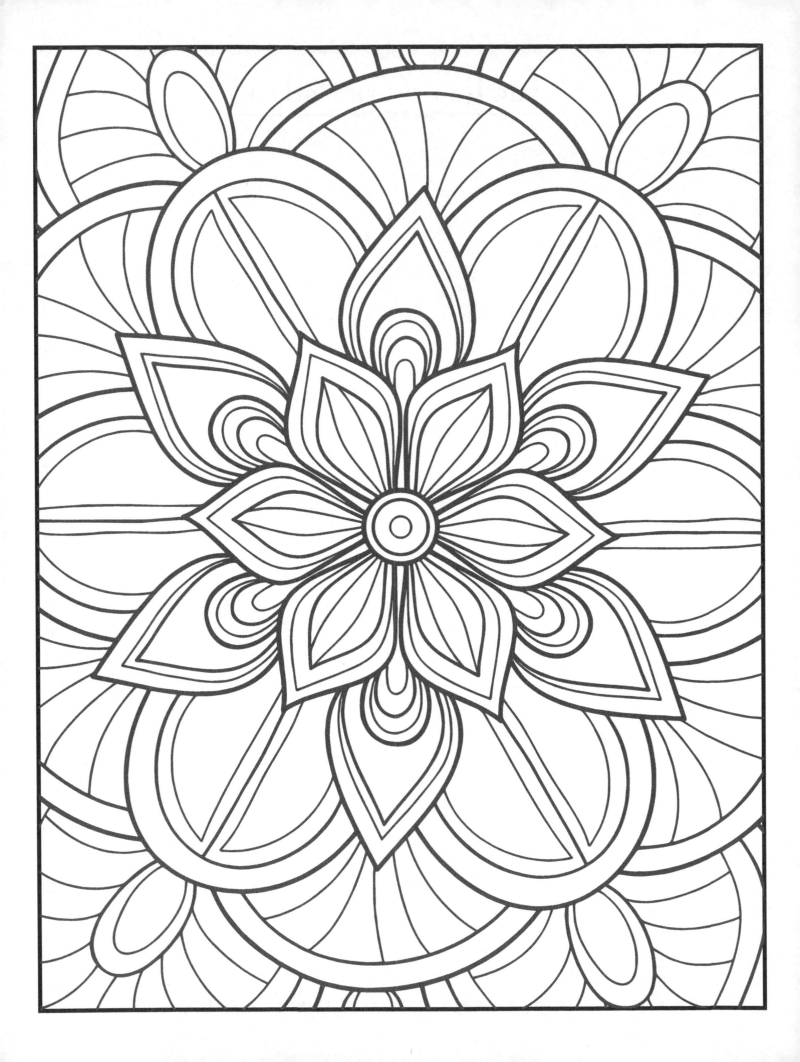

Create Your Own Patterns

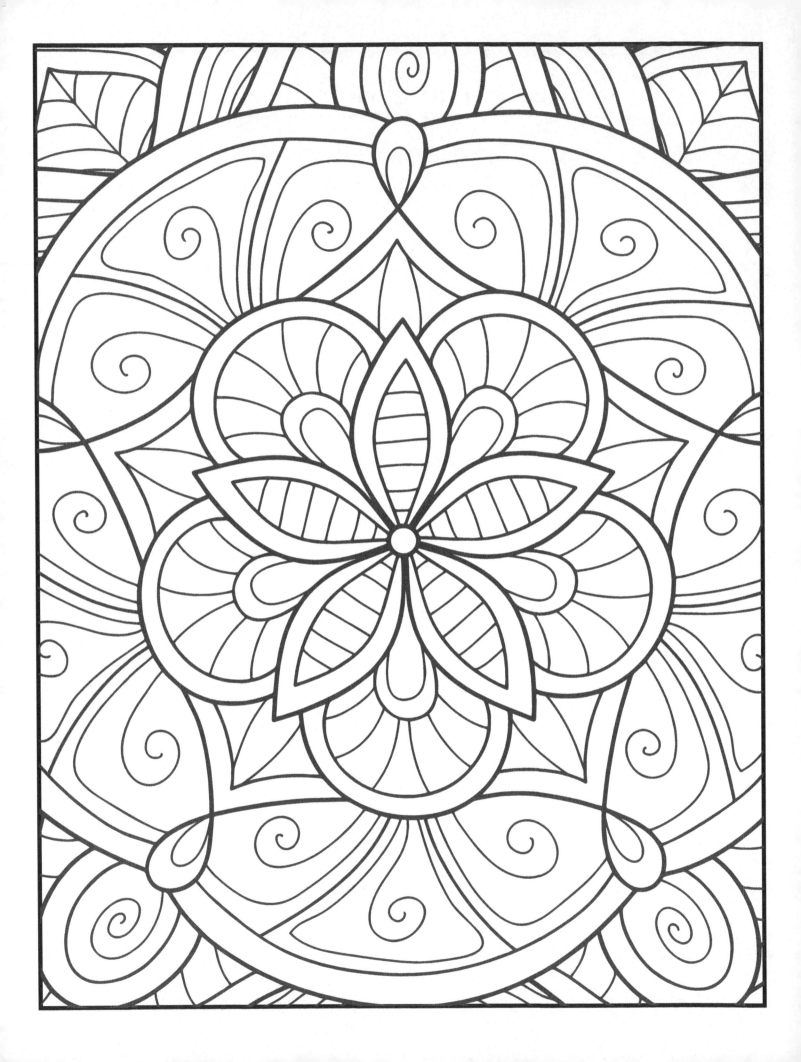

Create Your Own Patterns

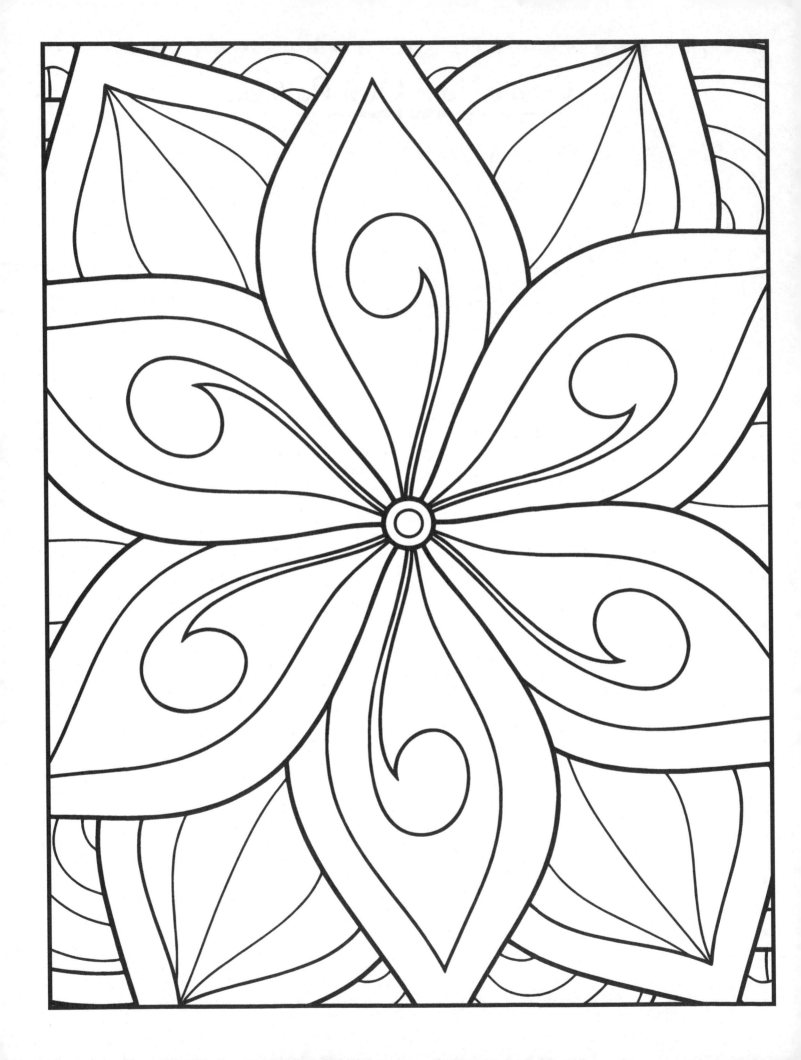

Create Your Own Patterns

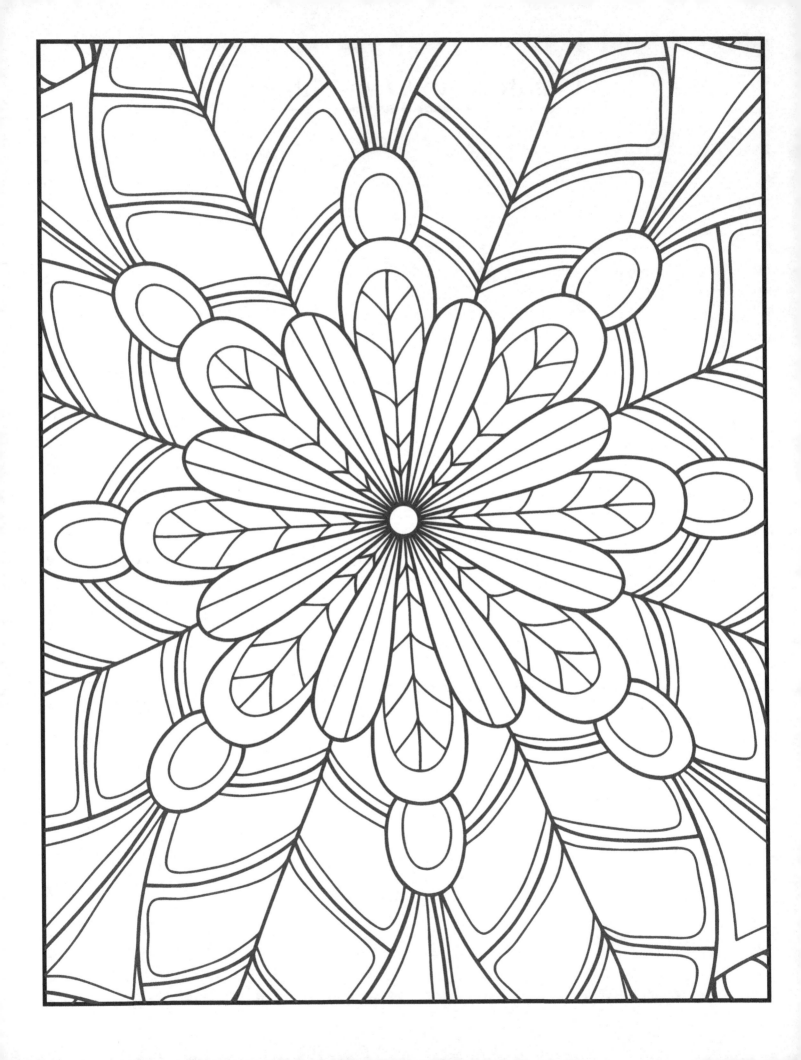

Create Your Own Patterns

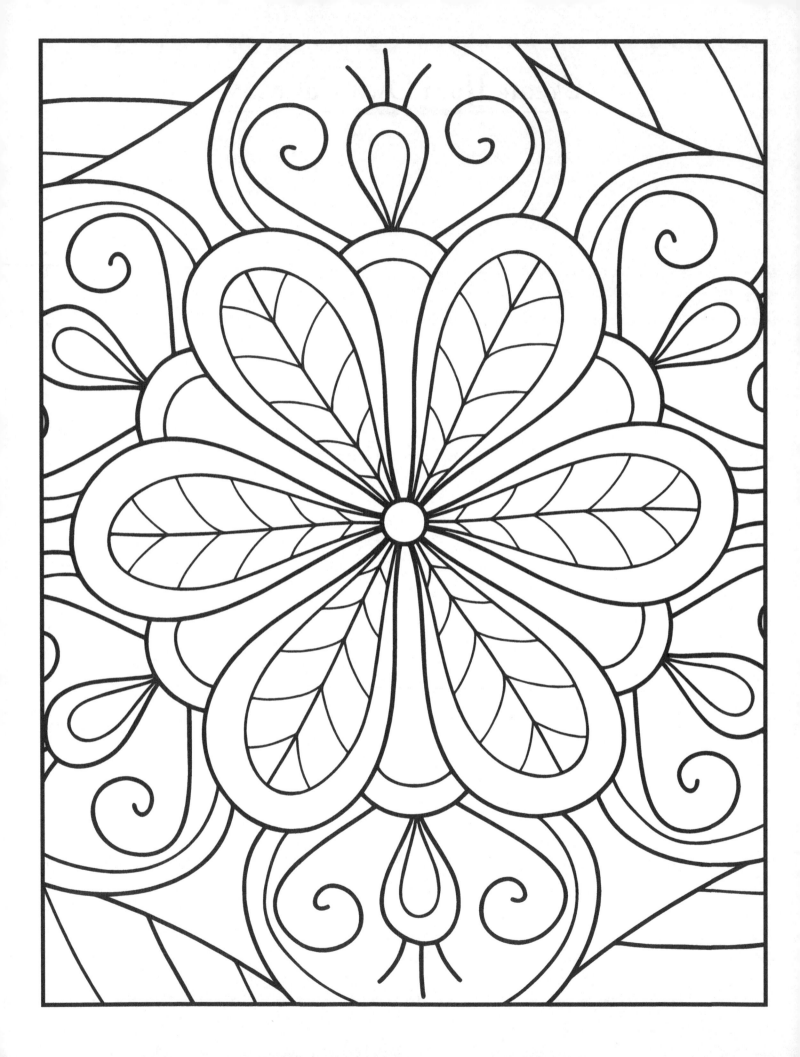

Create Your Own Patterns

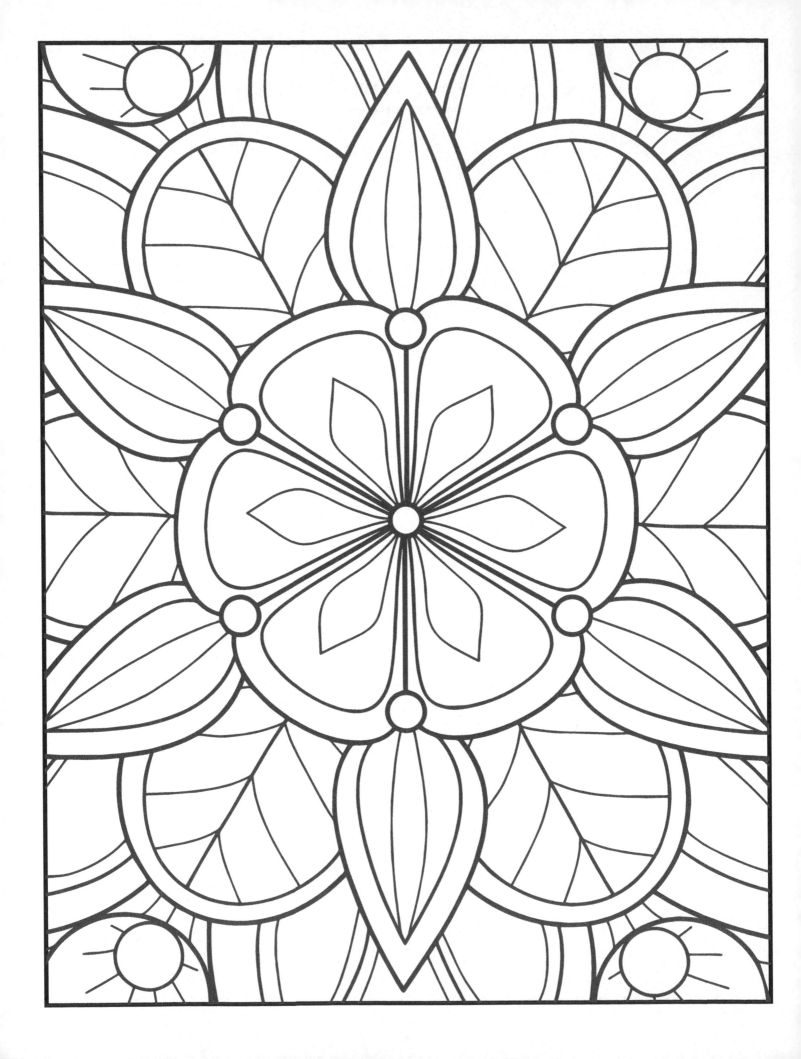

Create Your Own Patterns

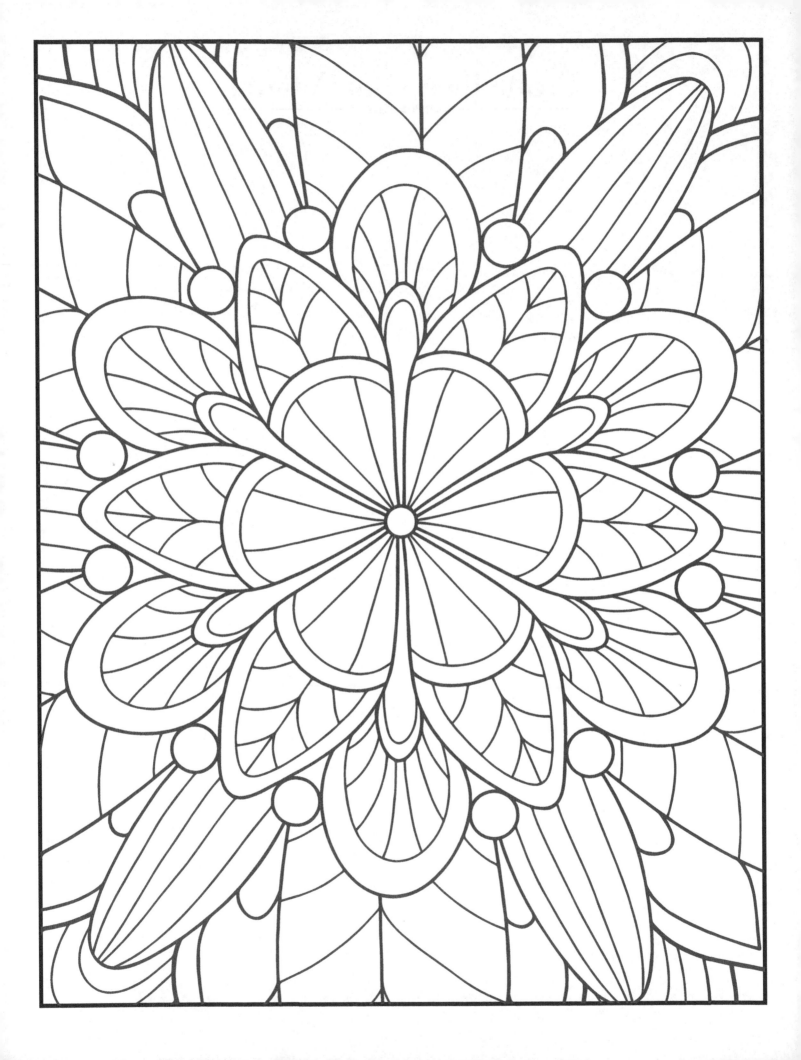

Create Your Own Patterns

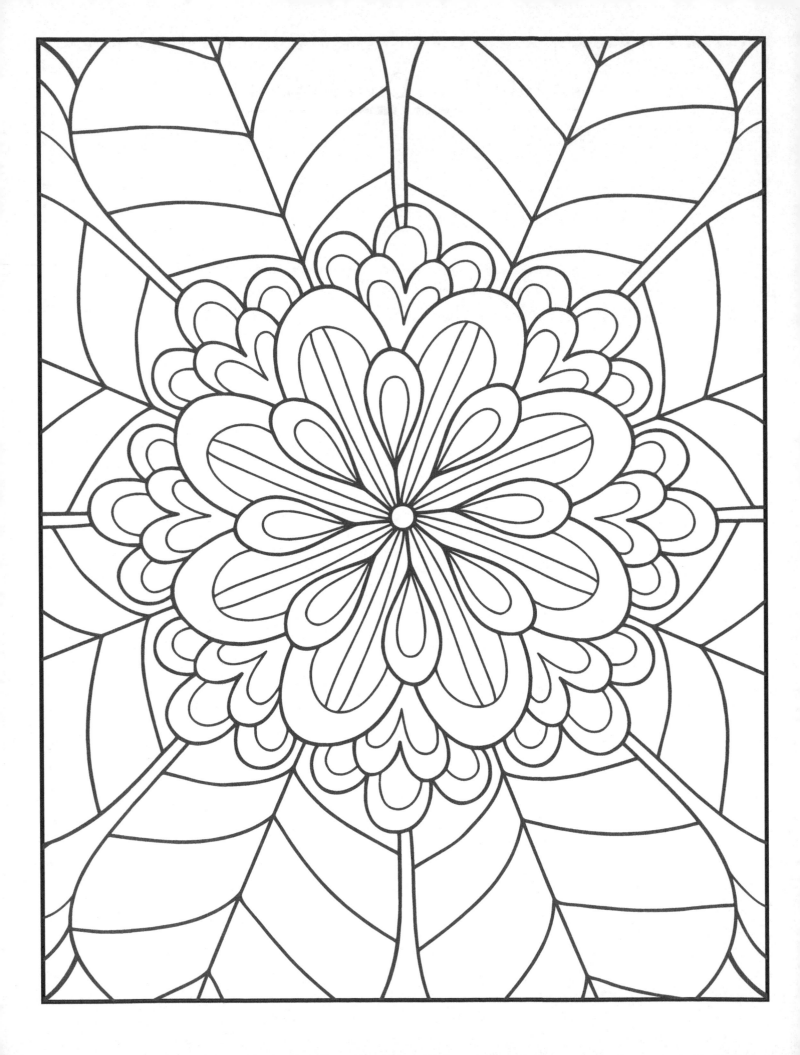

Create Your Own Patterns

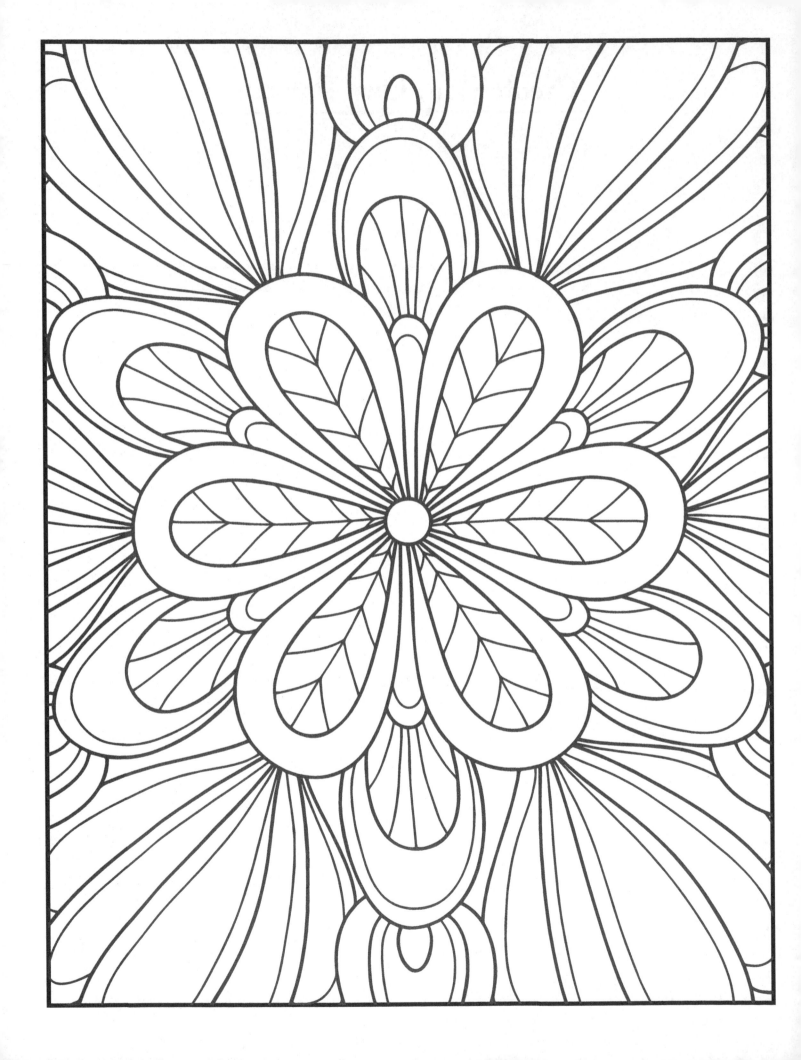

Create Your Own Patterns

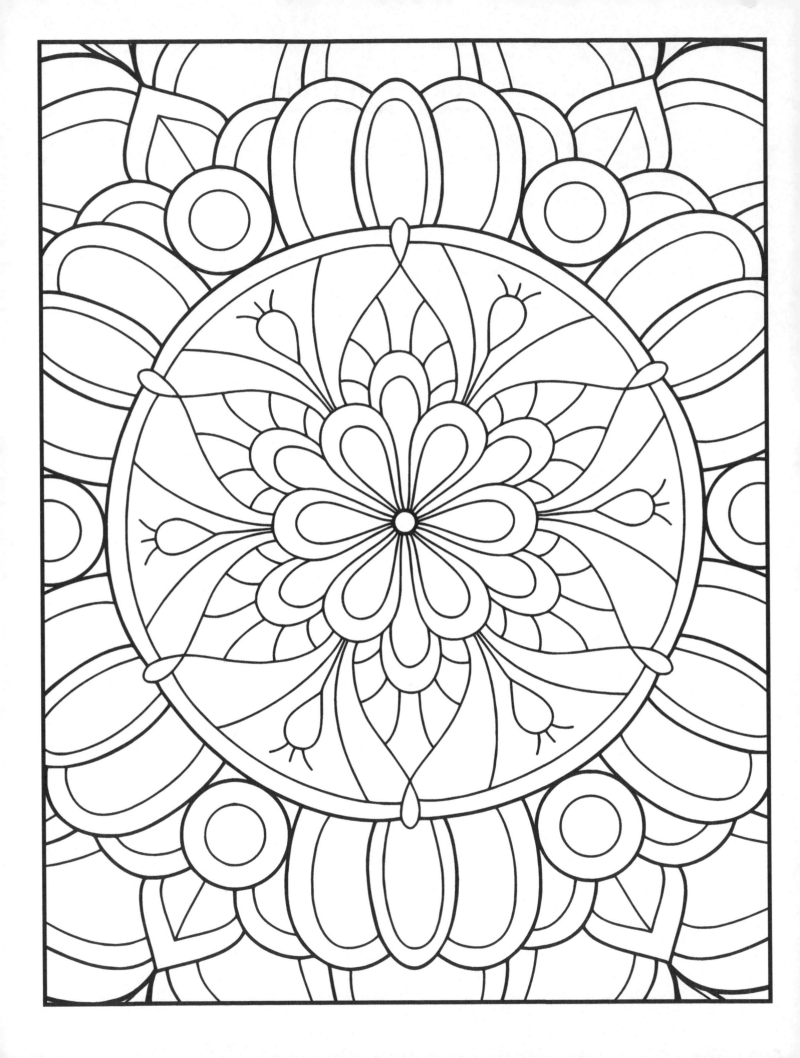

Create Your Own Patterns

Create Your Own Patterns

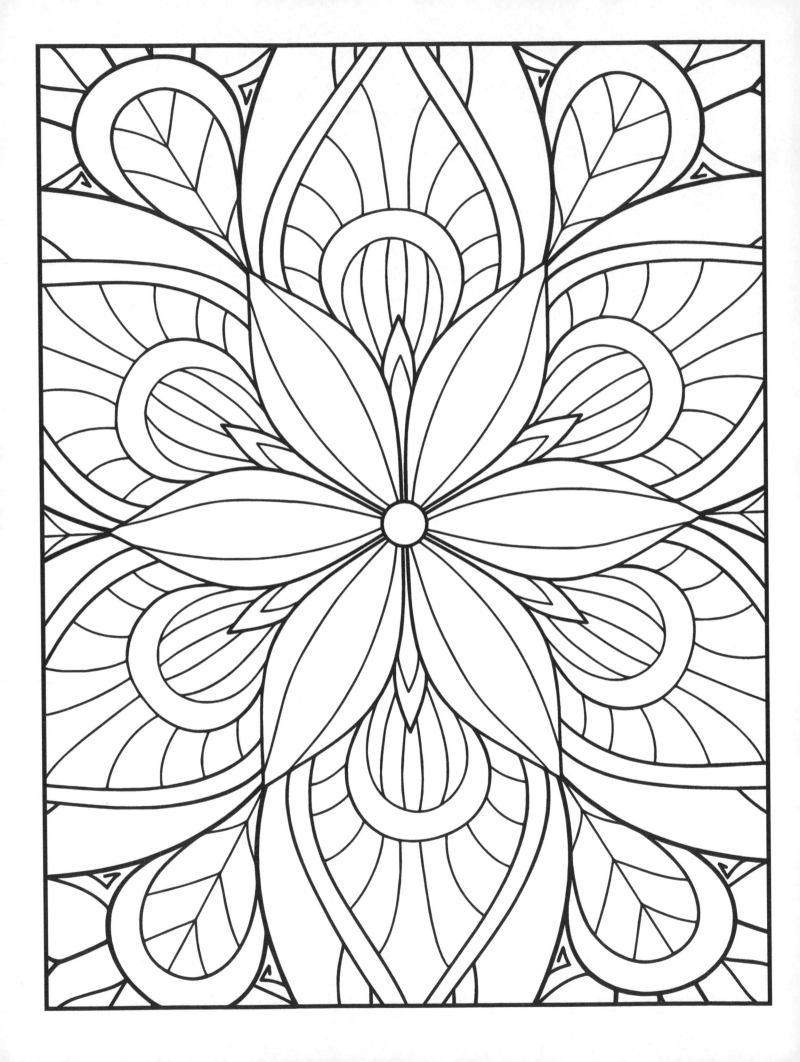

Create Your Own Patterns

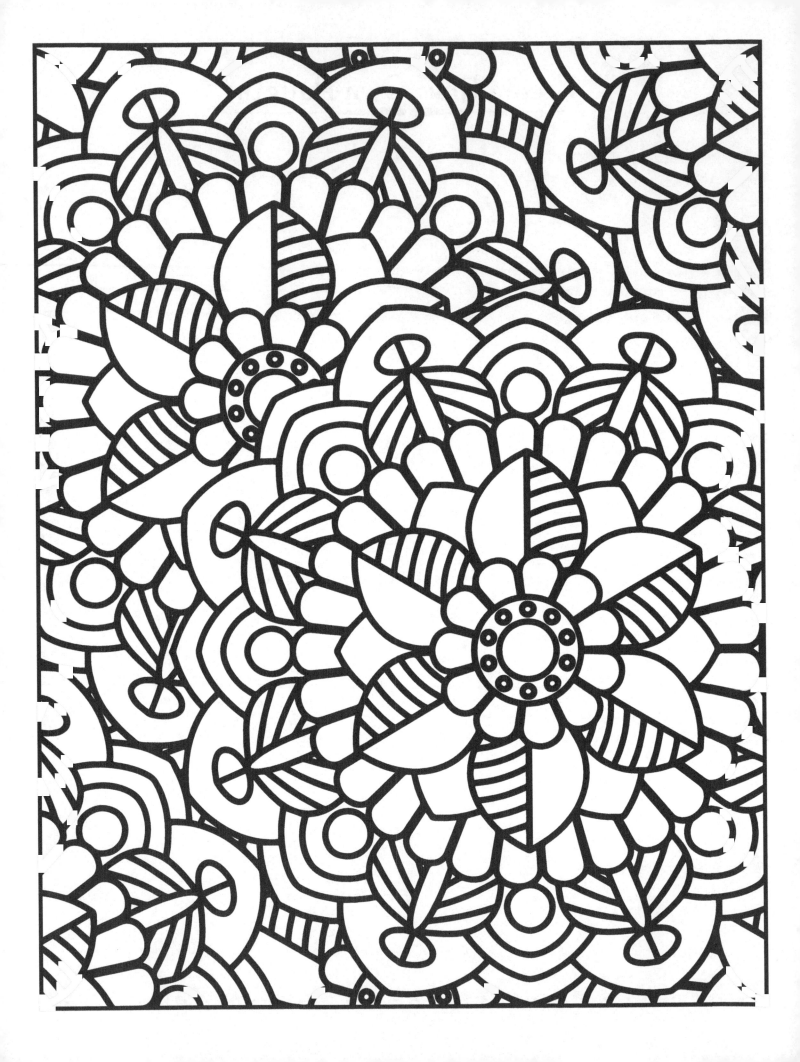

Create Your Own Patterns

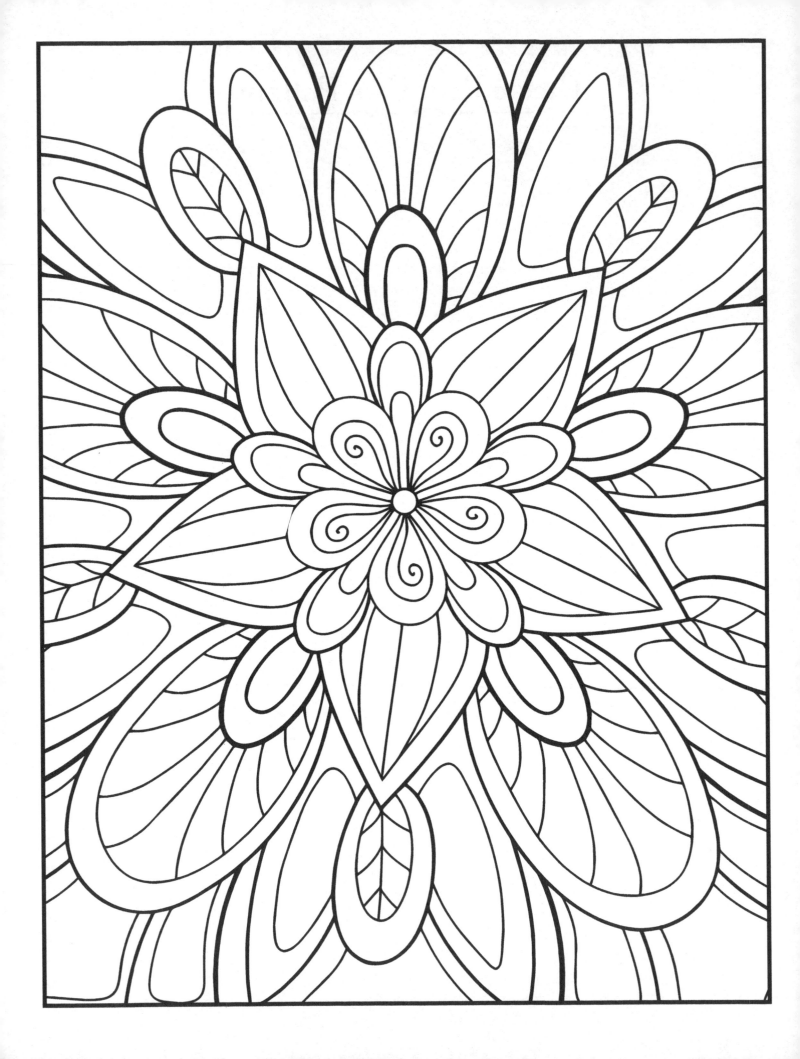

Create Your Own Patterns

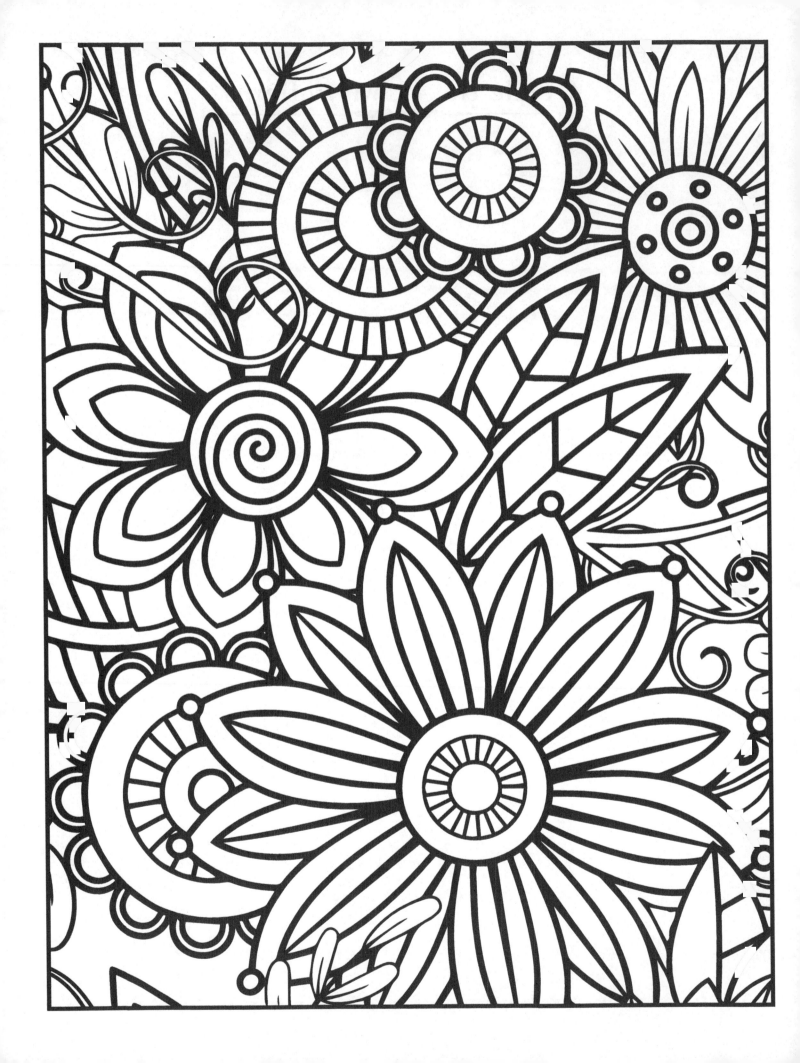

Create Your Own Patterns

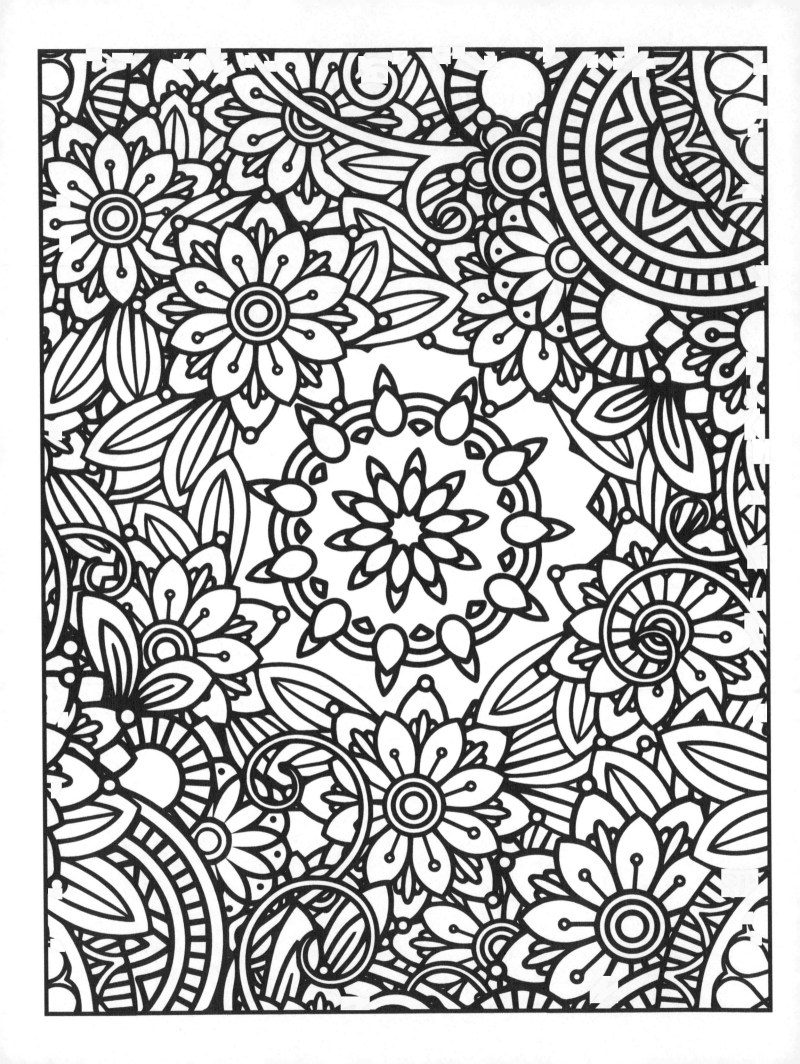

Create Your Own Patterns

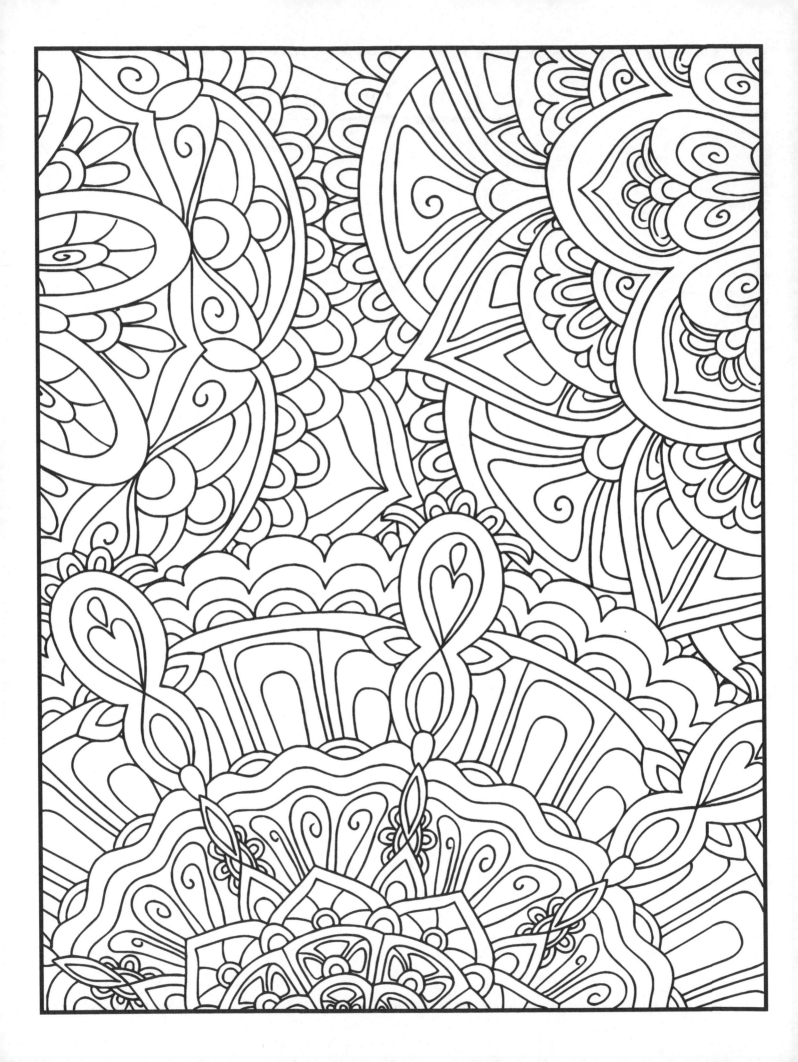

Create Your Own Patterns

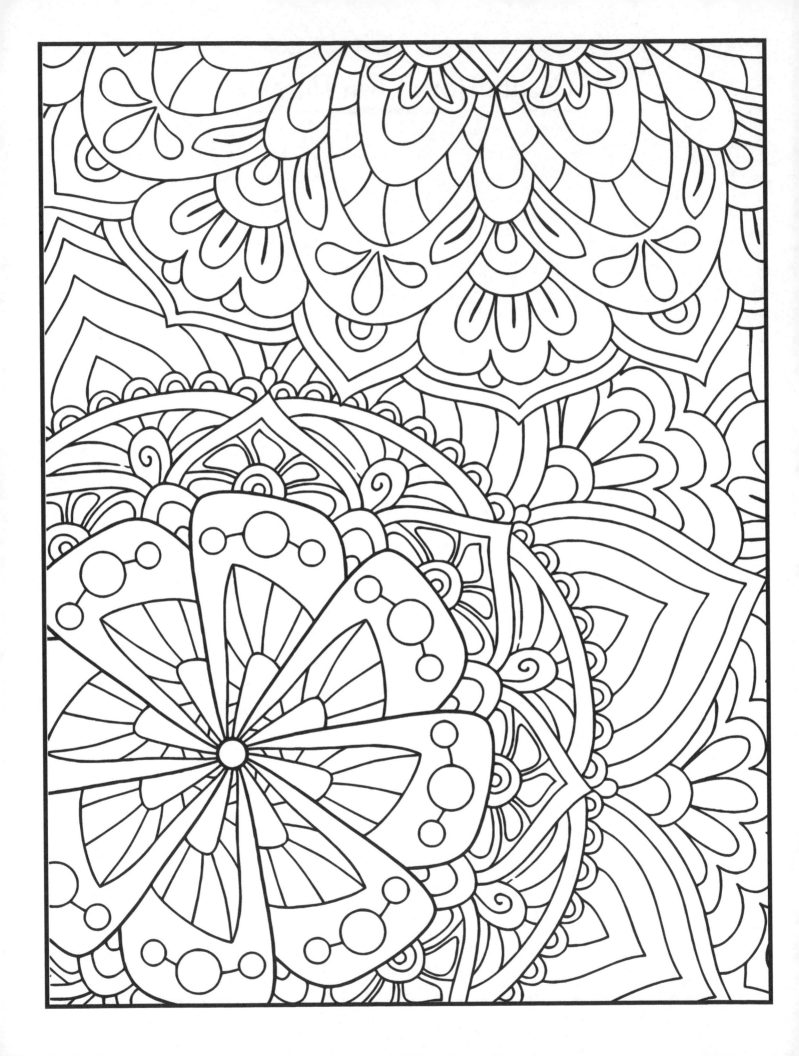

Create Your Own Patterns

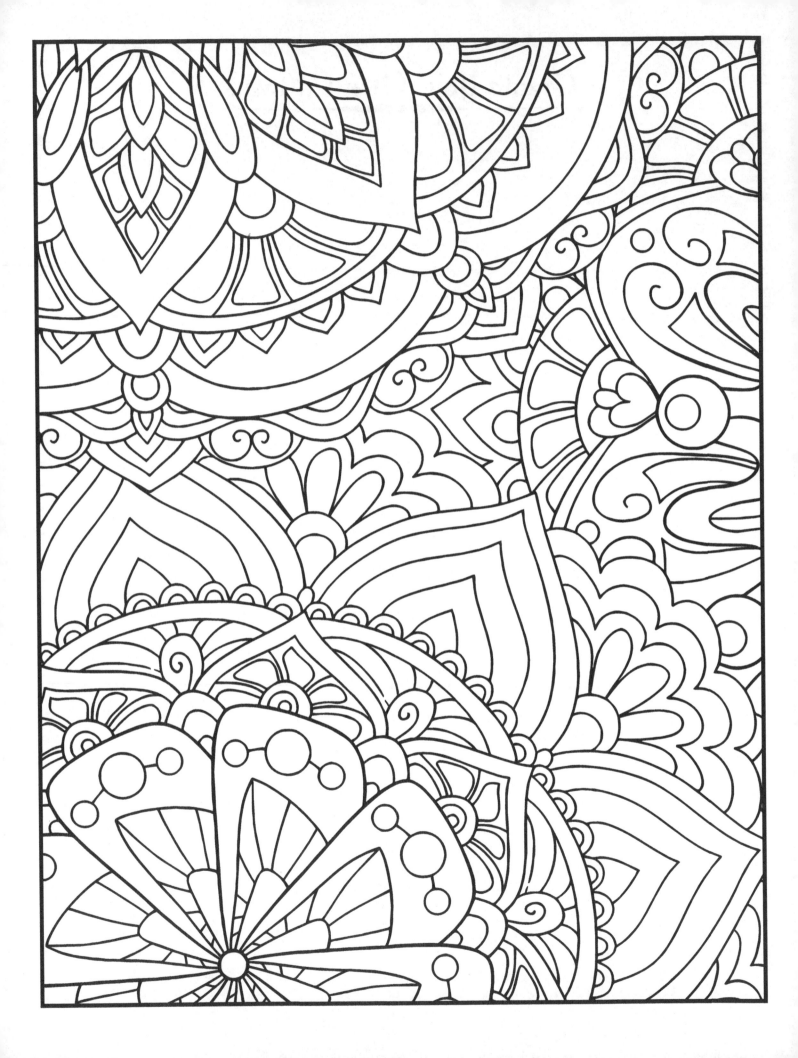

Create Your Own Patterns

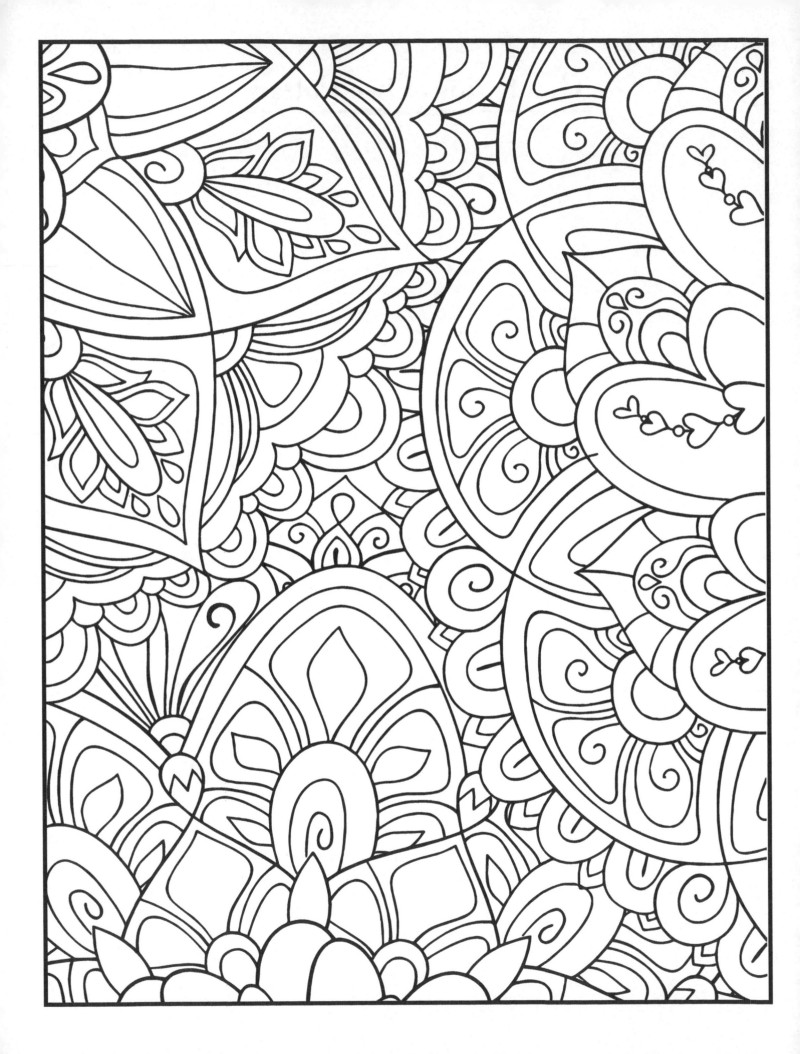

Create Your Own Patterns

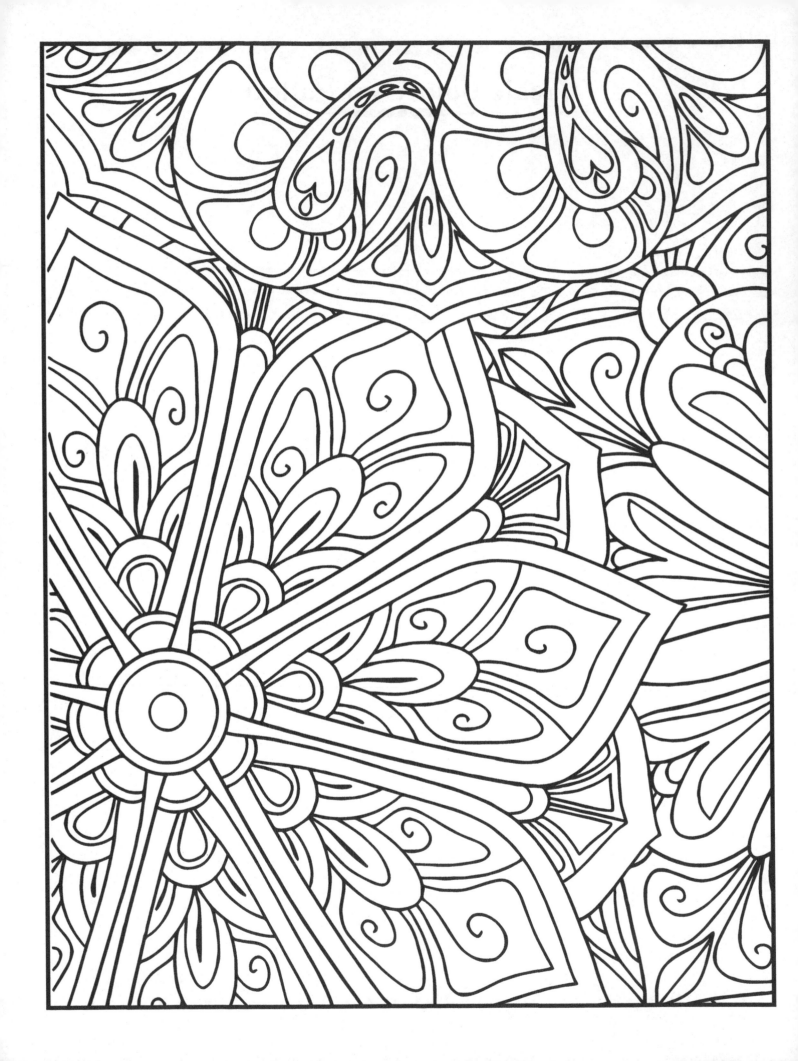

Create Your Own Patterns

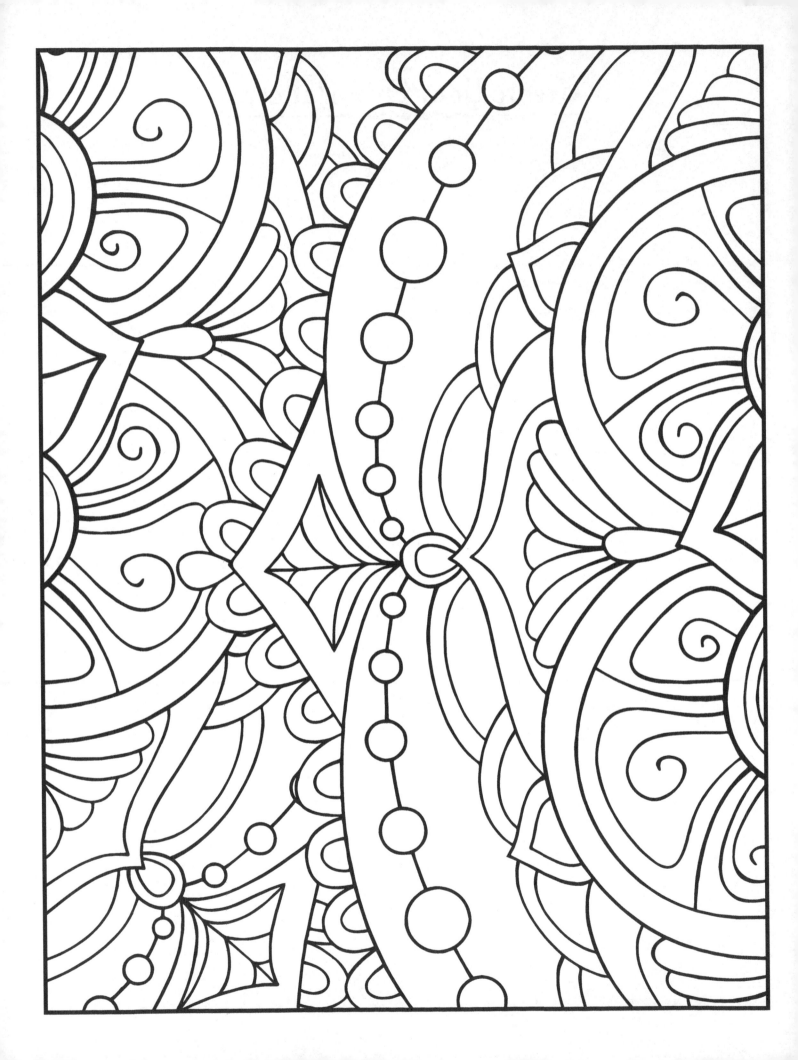

Create Your Own Patterns

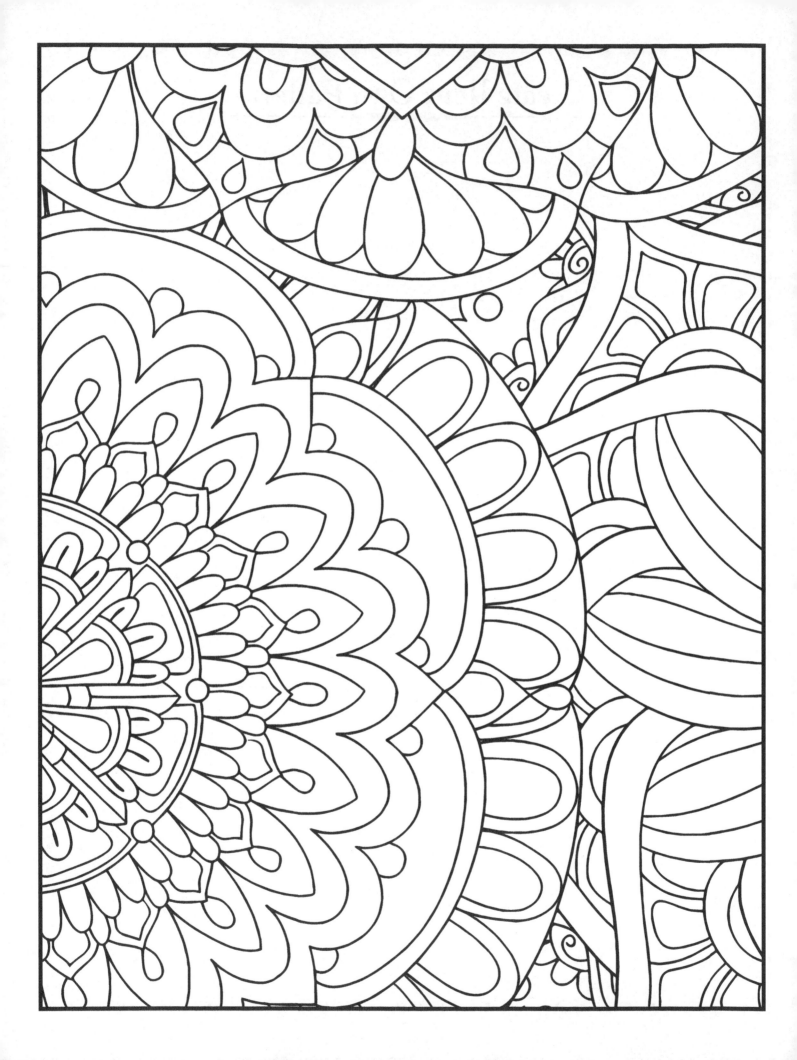

Create Your Own Patterns

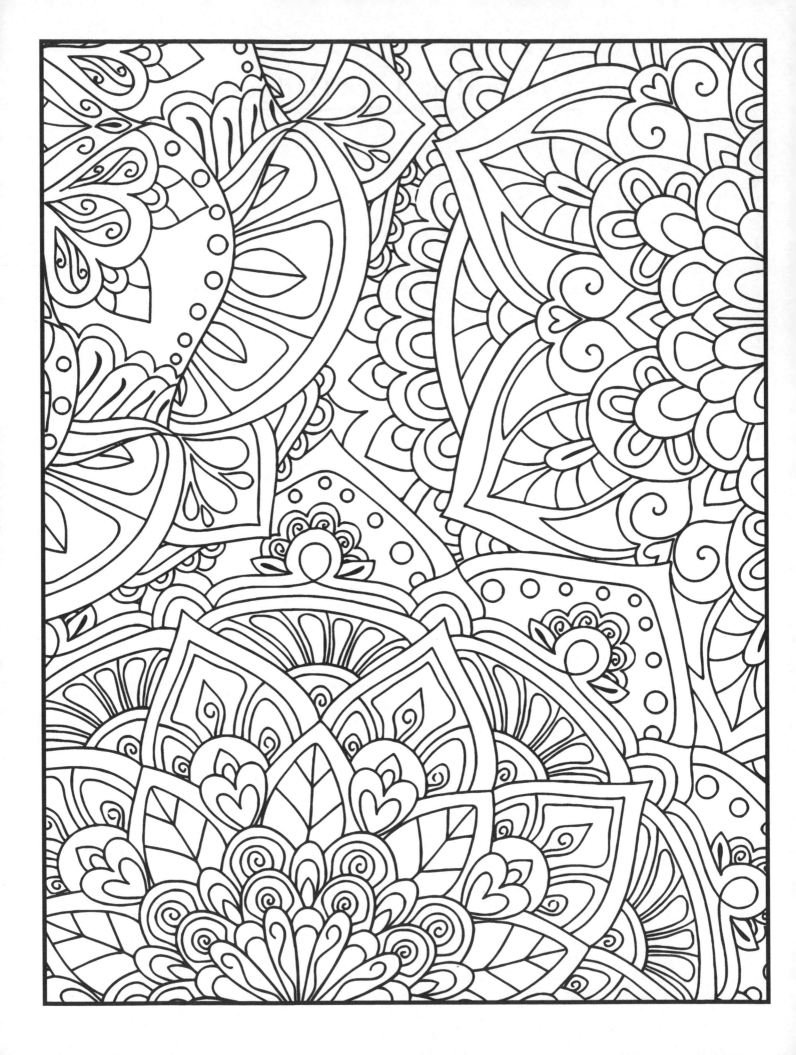

Create Your Own Patterns

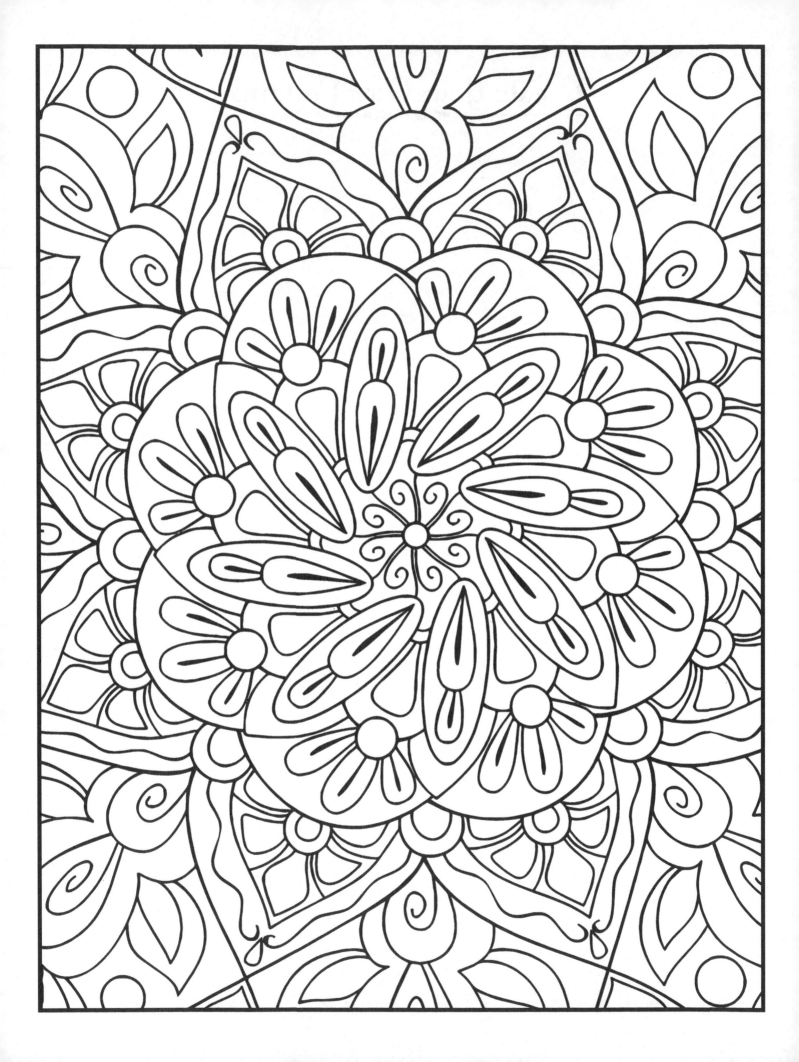

Create Your Own Patterns

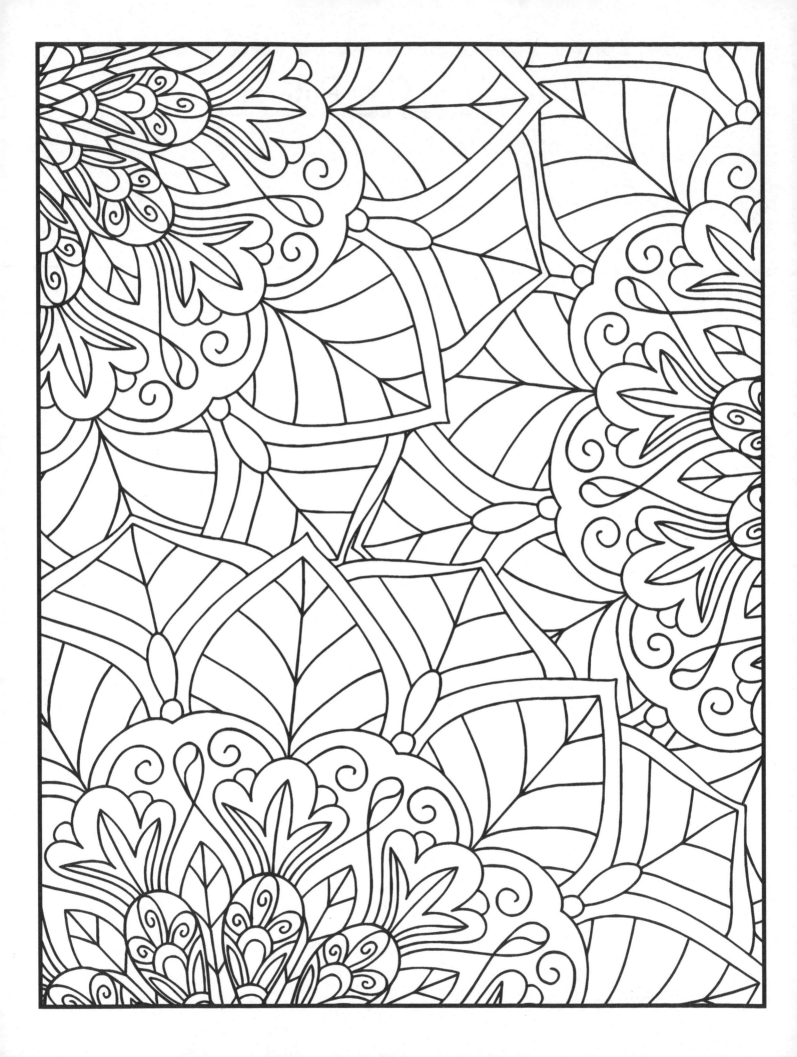

Create Your Own Patterns

Thank You!

We hope you enjoyed our book.

As a small family company, your feedback is very important to us.

Please let us know how you like our book at:

sophiejustincompany@gmail.com

Sophie Justin

71284107R00064